An
Ulster
Voice

In Search of Common Ground in Northern Ireland

Gary McMichael

94(
. G082x

FOREWORD BY Niall O'Dowd

ROBERTS RINEHART PUBLISHERS
Boulder, Colorado

Published by
Roberts Rinehart Publishers, 6309 Monarch Park Place, Niwot, Colorado 80503
Tel 303.652.2685 • Fax 303.652.2689 • www.robertsrinehart.com

Published in Ireland and the U.K. by
Roberts Rinehart Publishers, Trinity House, Charleston Road, Dublin 6

Distributed to the trade by Publishers Group West

International Standard Book Number 1-57098-275-9
Library of Congress Catalog Card Number 98-89916
Copyright © 1999 Gary McMichael

10 9 8 7 6 5 4 3 2 1

Book Design: Ann W. Douden, Boulder, Colorado

Typesetting: Red Barn Publishing, Skeagh, Skibbereen, Co. Cork

Author photo on pages 15, 73, 97, 131, 161 courtesy of Kelvin Boyes Photography

Manufactured in the United States of America

Contents

Part 4—1997   131

Part 5—1998   161

Acknowledgments

I would like to thank Jack Van Zandt for asking me to write this book and Niall O'Dowd for giving me the opportunity to share my views with others through his publications. My gratitude also goes to Bill Flynn for exposing Irish America to Loyalist voices. And, finally, I particularly want to thank Kirsten without whose hard work, encouragement and support this book would not have happened.

I also want to take this opportunity to pay tribute to John White, David Adams and my colleagues in the Ulster Democratic Party for their dedication in the pursuit of justice, equality and respect for the Loyalist community and for their commitment to bringing peace to all the people in Northern Ireland.

Above all, I want to thank my mother, for always being there.

Abbreviations

CLMC	–Combined Loyalist Military Command
DAAD	–Direct Action Against Drugs
DUP	–Democratic Unionist Party
INLA	–Irish National Liberation Army
IRA	–Irish Republican Army
IRSP	–Irish Republican Socialist Party
LVF	–Loyalist Volunteer Force
PUP	–Progressive Unionist Party
RUC	–Royal Ulster Constabulary
UDA	–Ulster Defence Association
UDP	–Ulster Democratic Party
UFF	–Ulster Freedom Fighters
UKUP	–UK Unionist Party
ULDP	–Ulster Loyalist Democratic Party
UUP	–Ulster Unionist Party

Foreword

The emergence of a powerful Loyalist political voice has been one of the most positive recent developments in Northern Ireland. At the head of the class of the new political thinkers has been Gary McMichael, leader of the Ulster Democratic Party, who has made a powerful impression on the body politic of the North.

Though still only in his twenties, McMichael has shown experience and political courage far beyond his years. I have seen him perform on stages as diverse as the White House and among his own constituency in Lisburn, where I accompanied him on a canvass during a recent election campaign.

In both cases, he equally impressed the high and mighty of Washington and the ordinary people of his district. Both clearly see him as a positive alternative to the negative voices of doom, which for too long have dominated large elements of Unionist politics.

His contribution to the new politics of Northern Ireland has been enormous. It should never be forgotten that, during the most tenuous phase of the Irish peace process, a majority of each community in Northern Ireland, as represented by their political parties, was necessary to agree the steps that led to the historic Good Friday Agreement.

On the Unionist side, there was a deep and almost even split among parties for and against compromise. It was Gary's Ulster Democratic Party and the other Loyalist group, the Progressive Unionist Party, who provided the crucial support for David Trimble's Ulster Unionist Party as they all edged towards an historic rapprochement.

It was an extraordinary risk for fledgling political parties to take and they were vilified in some Unionist quarters because of it. However, they showed extraordinary courage and imagination in sticking to the task they had set themselves and in

resisting the cat calls. There must have been a strong temptation at times just to row in behind the rigid old certainties, rather
than to strike out towards new but risky possibilities. I know that
was a tense and often lonely time for Gary as his party faced
much derision and abuse for taking their courage in their hands
and voting for historic compromises. His dream of a new departure where the two communities in Northern Ireland could
progress together is now close to fulfilment. Unfortunately, his
party is not part of the new assembly, as it faces the growing
pains which any new political grouping must deal with. However, he is more determined than ever to build on the solid grassroots support that they enjoy and to expand their political base.

Gary's role is all the more extraordinary, given his own personal background. He had every reason to grow up bitter and
to become ripe fodder for paramilitary recruitment, given that
his father was killed by the IRA. Instead he chose another path,
one far more honorable and courageous, and one that, I believe,
will eventually see him as one of the major political figures in
Northern Ireland.

His father, John McMichael, forged many links with Irish
Americans, particularly with the legendary Paul O'Dwyer, the
fiery civil rights lawyer. From that association came many of the
progressive and far-seeing policies of the Ulster Democratic
Party, first represented in their document "Commonsense."

When the Irish American peace delegation of which I was
a member first began visiting Northern Ireland, we found in
Gary and his associates like David Adams a ready willingness
to hear and entertain the American perspective on the Irish
problem.

Indeed, the openness of the two Loyalist paramilitary parties to American opinion was one of the most striking and hope-
ful outcomes of our many visits there. We realized that, for too
long, Loyalist opinion had been overlooked in America and not
given its proper weight in the Unionist equation. We determined to change that.

As part of that outreach, Gary began writing for my weekly newspaper, the *Irish Voice*. His columns came as a shock to

many of my readers, accustomed as they were to the old ortho-
doxies that Unionism or Loyalism had nothing new to say.

His columns repeatedly challenged the easy assumptions
that many Irish Americans have about such matters. This is,
after all, a country that has been too long exposed to the Reverend Ian Paisley and his type and not long enough to saner
Unionist political voices.

Gary's columns have become a popular feature of our newspaper and, through the past few years of historic breakthroughs
and developments, we are proud to have offered a forum both
to him and Gerry Adams, the Sinn Féin leader, to express views
long censored or overlooked in America.

As you read this book of columns, remember the bravery
and integrity shown by Gary and his fellow party members
when they stood for change, when it would have been much
easier to accept the status quo in Northern Ireland. When the
history of this period is documented, I have no doubt that the
name of Gary McMichael will be writ large indeed. This book
is a testament to his courage.

Niall O'Dowd
Founding Publisher
Irish Voice Newspaper
December 14, 1998

Introduction
by
Kirsten E. Schulze

Kirsten E. Schulze is Lecturer in International History at the London School of Economics, and is currently writing a book on Loyalist political development and military strategy.

The Northern Ireland conflict has often been portrayed as one between the Irish people and the British state, as the fight of the Irish Republican Army (IRA) against the last vestiges of British colonialism. The story of the conflict most often told is one of British military occupation, discrimination against Catholics by Protestants, domination by Unionists, oppression, and human rights abuses. This account, however, is not only somewhat inaccurate, as the conflict is really one of competing nationalisms – British and Irish; Unionist and Nationalist – it is also highly selective. As the Northern Ireland conflict has many fault-lines, only one of which is the British state–Republican struggle, there is also more than one narrative of the conflict. This book compiled of Loyalist politician Gary McMichael's articles shares the experience of the Loyalist community in its efforts to defend the Union and its search for equality, common ground and, ultimately, peace.

The Loyalist story of the conflict in Northern Ireland is not one of domination, but one of poverty, disenfranchisement, and marginalization. It is the story of the Protestant working-class community, which has been on the front-line of the conflict by virtue of sharing the poorer neighborhoods of Belfast, Lisburn and Portadown as well as rural mid-Ulster with the Catholic working class. As a result, Loyalists have had a similar experience to that of Republicans. And, equally, many Loyalists supported paramilitary organizations, seeing violence as a way of empowering the community. Yet, at the same time, they remained trapped throughout most of the conflict as their struggle for political, economic and social equality was subordinated to the defense of the Union, a situation which only started to change with the onset of the peace process in 1994.

Before looking at some of the key events in the Loyalist history of the conflict, some general remarks about Unionism need to be made. As Loyalists are Unionists, they have suffered from the same historic insecurities about the constitutional position of what today is Northern Ireland. Unionists throughout history have been loyal to the monarchy as the embodiment of their Britishness, yet their loyalty towards the government in Westminster has always been of a more conditional nature. This conditionality was based on the fear, especially in the nineteenth and twentieth centuries, that their government would sell them out if politically expedient. The Home Rule debate in the latter part of the nineteenth century and the still prevalent attitude in mainland Britain that the Unionists are "not really British" have served to underline this belief. Indeed, the perception that Northern Ireland was only allowed to remain part of the United Kingdom after the First World War because of Ulster's sacrifice on the battlefields of Flanders is widespread and not necessarily unfounded. This has meant that, while Unionists wanted to trust their government to protect them, historical experience has taught them not to do so. In fact, from the massacres of 1641 onwards, there has been a strong Unionist tradition for establishing self-defense organizations ranging from small public bands to a full army, the Ulster Volunteer Force in 1912. The Loyalist paramilitary organizations, which arose within the context of the 1969 Troubles, are also part of this tradition.

Unionist insecurity has not only been the result of British ambiguity, but also of being a minority on the island of Ireland. This is a factor that is often overlooked when considering the conflict in Northern Ireland in which the minority so clearly seems to be a Catholic Nationalist one. Within the broader context of Anglo-Irish history, however, there have been two religious minorities – the Catholics in the United Kingdom of Great

Britain and Ireland before partition and in Northern Ireland after partition, as well as the Protestants, and particularly the non-ascendancy Presbyterians, in Ireland. Each minority's fear of domination by the other has thus pre-determined their actions and reactions to a large extent. Ulster Protestants throughout Anglo-Irish history perceived themselves to be a minority under threat, even after they became a majority in Northern Ireland after partition. They supported partition and continue to oppose Irish unification as they were not and are not prepared to become a minority in an Irish Catholic state. The emergence of militant Irish Nationalism and the formation of the IRA to pursue a unification of Ireland by force, only served to reinforce Protestant fears and the feeling of embattledness. In light of this siege mentality, it is not surprising that attempts to resolve the conflict from 1969 onwards, were all viewed suspiciously by the Unionist population. Each initiative was inspected meticulously for indications that the British government had decided to get rid of Northern Ireland once and for all.

When the partition of Ireland was formalized by the 1920 Government of Ireland Act and the 1921 Anglo-Irish Treaty, neither Catholics nor Protestants had achieved their desired aims. While northern Catholics longed for a united Ireland, Protestants feared the devolved position of Northern Ireland within the United Kingdom was yet another way for Westminster to wash its hands of the whole Irish question. The Nationalist response to partition was not to participate in the new state structures and thus legitimize them by becoming the official opposition. The Unionist middle class, after initially feeling betrayed by Westminster, seized the opportunity to establish what is often referred to as the "Orange State," "Protestant State," or simply Stormont, which clearly excluded the Catholic Nationalist population. In practical terms, however, the new Northern Ireland also excluded the Loyalists, marginalizing them socially, politically and economically.

As a result, every-day life for the Protestant working class did not differ greatly from that of the Catholic working class.

While there certainly were significantly more Protestants employed in the shipyards and factories than Catholics, and Catholic "disloyalists" had been driven out of factories and mills, the difference in living conditions and political partic-ipation was a matter of degree rather than substance. Neither had the right to vote in local elections as the franchise was restricted to rate payers, property occupation, and businesses. Unionist politicians did not attempt to include either in the decision-making process. Both were pushed to the fringes of society and, on the whole, they were as economically impov-erished as other working-class populations in Europe at that time. Indeed, it could be argued that the only advantage the Loyalist community had over its Republican counterpart was that of being exploited or neglected by a political elite it con-sidered to be its own.

The majority of families in Loyalist areas lived in terrace houses in squalid conditions, without proper heating or inside toilets. The effects of poverty were further exacerbated by periodic sectarian clashes and violence along interface areas. Most youngsters dropped out of school early to work in the shipyards of Harland and Wolff or in the linen industry. How-ever, when the Depression hit Northern Ireland in 1930, one third of industrial workers became unemployed and in 1932, many within the Loyalist community were on the verge of starvation. In 1938, unemployment had reached 29.5 percent. The outbreak of the Second World War temporarily halted Northern Ireland's industrial decline, but added the burden of rationing and air raids. After the war, employment contin-ued to fall, dropping from 65,000 to 19,000 in the textile indus-try and from 24,000 to 10,000 in shipbuilding between 1950 and 1973. And more and more Loyalists joined the growing ranks of the unemployed.

When the Northern Ireland Civil Rights Association (NICRA) was formed on February 1, 1967, many of its aims should have struck a chord within the Loyalist community. The fact, however, that several prominent NICRA members were Republican, made many Protestants believe that the civil rights movement was just a front for a united Ireland. Consequently, Loyalists, who would have benefited from reform, felt compelled to protest against the civil rights campaign and to hold on to a form of government which had not served them particularly well, in order to protect the Union.

The perception that civil rights really meant Nationalist rights was further strengthened when the reforms initiated in response only addressed deprived Nationalist areas. Thus, what Loyalists saw from across the religious divide were new houses and improved education opportunities for Catholics only. Here was their Unionist leadership, never having shared its economic and political prosperity with its own working class, handing out benefits to the enemy. And here was the Protestant working class, which had never swayed in its loyalty to the Union, trapped between wanting social equality and not being able even to raise the issue for fear of playing into Republican hands.

Loyalist protest against the Civil Rights Movement combined with the rising fear of a Republican military challenge could not and did not prevent Northern Ireland from imploding. In July and August 1969, sectarian riots started to spread throughout Belfast and Derry. Catholic working-class areas erected barricades and "no-go" areas for the police, and neighboring Protestant working-class areas increasingly perceived themselves and Northern Ireland as a whole to be under threat. This perception was compounded by the dissolution of the Ulster Special Constabulary or "B-Specials" on April 30, 1970, which in their eyes left them defenseless in the face of the emerging military campaign of the newly formed, more radical Provisional IRA.

The belief that the security forces were no longer able adequately to protect Loyalist areas from Republican attack led to the formation of a number of local vigilante groups, which were united into the Ulster Defense Association (UDA) in September 1971. The UDA quickly assumed the manning of barricades and the patroling of Loyalist areas, as Northern Ireland's deathtoll rose from 25 in 1970 to 174 in 1971; shootings increased from 213 to 1,756; and the number of bombs went from 170 to 1,515. The breakdown of law and order seemed imminent by the end of the year.

The deterioration of the security situation was soon followed by the collapse of the political one. On March 24, 1972, Conservative Prime Minister Edward Heath announced the suspension of the Stormont government. Direct rule from Westminster was extended over Northern Ireland in an attempt to provide for a fresh start and to find a political solution to the conflict. The abolition of Stormont created a considerable amount of anxiety within the Unionist community. Hopes, however, that direct rule would translate into full integration into the United Kingdom and the end of Northern Ireland's status as "a place apart," soon gave way to an overwhelming sense of fear that direct rule was the first step to casting Northern Ireland out of the Union.

The brunt of the disarray within Unionism and the continuing sectarian strife was borne by the Loyalist community. The UDA's membership increased to an estimated 40–50,000 men and women, making it the largest paramilitary organization in Northern Ireland. The membership of the more secretive UVF, which had been re-established in 1966 to counter a Republican resurgence in response to the fiftieth anniversary of the Easter Rising, also grew. Both paramilitaries attempted to fill the security gap by protecting Loyalist areas through acts of retaliation against neighboring Republican or Nationalist areas. Yet, like the victims of many Republican attacks in the early days of the conflict who were killed because they happened to be in shopping areas, bus stations, or Protestant neighborhoods, the victims of Loyalist paramilitaries often were guilty only of being Catholic or living on the Falls Road.

The first initiative to resolve the conflict following the extension of direct rule came with the 1973 elections for a new Northern Ireland assembly. The run-up to the elections was characterized by an increase in violence and the emergence of a new Loyalist paramilitary factor, the Ulster Freedom Fighters (UFF), a more secretive grouping under the umbrella of the UDA. At the same time, hope for change never ceased. Indeed, 72.3 percent of the electorate went to the polls in an attempt to make a difference. Expectations of an end to the conflict, however, were dashed when the new assembly announced the creation of a Unionist–Nationalist power-sharing executive on November 22. This provoked Loyalist anger, based on the belief that sharing power with politicians whose goal was a united Ireland could only lead in one direction – out of the United Kingdom. The decision by those politicians in the executive to exclude Loyalists from the Sunningdale Conference, which had been convened to address the conflict, was the final nail in the coffin. Loyalists once again had been marginalized and excluded from the democratic process. They were being forced into accepting an executive composed of individuals who had brought down the Stormont government and who were hailing the establishment of the Council of Ireland under the Sunningdale Agreement as a stepping stone towards a united Ireland.

Within this context of a perceived "sell-out," Loyalists started organizing a broad opposition to the new power-sharing executive, drafting in disaffected Unionists, Paisleyites, trade unionists and the paramilitaries. On March 23, 1974, the newly formed Loyalist Ulster Workers' Council (UWC) threatened wide-spread civil disobedience unless new assembly elections were held. On May 15, the UWC strike began with power cuts and factory closures, while roads were barricaded by the paramilitaries. Unionist grass-roots support for the strike ensured that Northern Ireland indeed came to a standstill, despite the State of Emergency and British Army attempts to break the strike. And, ultimately, the power-sharing executive was brought down by militant Loyalism.

This militarization of the Loyalist community in the 1970s resulted in a number of political shifts which marked the first hesitant steps on the road to political emancipation. A sizable segment of the Loyalist community started to vote for Ian Paisley's Democratic Unionist Party (DUP) rather than the Ulster Unionist Party (UUP), which they had traditionally supported.

The combination of Paisley's hard-line rhetoric with his attempt to address working-class issues, appealed to many Loyalist voters. They had become disillusioned with middle-class Unionist politicians only ever showing their faces on the Shankill Road at election time. They also had lost trust in a Unionist elite which had been part of the power-sharing executive. By bringing down this executive through the 1974 Ulster Workers' Council strike, they had flexed their muscle. This empowerment sowed the seeds for repeated attempts to establish distinctly Loyalist political parties so that Loyalist interests would no longer be neglected by Unionist politicians. These efforts, however, foundered because the majority of Protestants still preferred to vote for "respectable" DUP candidates who were not associated with violence over those of a paramilitary background. Thus most of the early attempts at going political were nipped in the bud. In the end, the failure of Loyalists to seize the reins immediately after the UWC strike and the inability to break into the political arena, set back the politicization of the Loyalist paramilitaries for another decade.

If the key events shaping Loyalist military strategy and political development in the 1970s were the collapse of law and order, direct rule and the Ulster Workers' strike, the main influences in the 1980s arguably were the hunger strikes and Sinn Féin's consequent political gains, as well as the Anglo-Irish Agreement.

On April 1, 1980, the British government abolished the special status category for all Loyalist and Republican prisoners in an attempt to criminalize politically motivated offenses and thus undermine popular support for the paramilitaries. This policy of criminalization was met by protest, as it not only meant prison uniforms and restriction on movement and association, but also denied that violence could be in any way politically motivated. On October 27, seven Republican H-Block prisoners started one of many hunger strikes demanding the right to wear their own clothes, the freedom of association with other prisoners and to organize their own recreation facilities. The strike was followed by "dirty protests" and "going on the blanket." Full impact, however, was not achieved until the hunger strike begun by Bobby Sands on March 1, 1981 – a strike, which ultimately cost him his life on May 5, but not until after he had won the Fermanagh-South Tyrone Westminster by-election on April 9.

Loyalist prisoners sympathized with Republican demands to reinstate special status, which would have effectively recognized them as political prisoners as well. They could not, however, be seen to cooperate with Republicans, especially since the British government – their government – was portraying the protest as an attempt to legitimize IRA terrorism. Loyalists were thus caught between a rock and a hard place. They saw the detrimental effects of the "criminalization" of the conflict, yet loyalty demanded that they support their government. What they also saw was a Nationalist community, which supported Republican prisoners, and a Unionist community, which went to lengths to dissociate itself from Loyalist prisoners. Consequently, while the hunger strikes empowered the Republican community, it had the opposite effect on the Loyalist community, increasing the sense of betrayal, abandonment and marginalization as once again the conflict had slid into an IRA–British state dynamic.

International support, the rise of Catholic Nationalism and, finally, the election of hunger-striker Bobby Sands set in motion two important processes within Loyalism. First, Loyalists realized that Sinn Féin would reap the political benefits from the hunger strikes. This reinvigorated the process of politicization of the Loyalist paramilitaries, resulting in the UDA's creation of the Ulster Loyalist Democratic Party (ULDP) in 1981 as well as the integration of Loyalist political and military strategies. The second process initiated was a shift in the military thinking of Loyalist prisoners in particular from reactiveness to pro-activeness, from defense to offense – leading to a shift in strategy once these prisoners had been released and moved into leadership positions in the late 1980s.

The 1985 Anglo-Irish Agreement reinforced both these processes. The fact that the Agreement had been signed by the

British and Irish governments without even an attempt at consulting the people in Northern Ireland and the fact that there now was an institutionalized "Irish dimension" increased the Unionist and Loyalist perception of betrayal. The extent and depth of this feeling becomes clear when looking at some of the statements from Unionist politicians at that time. For example, Unionist MP Harold McCusker told the House of Commons, "I stood outside Hillsborough, not waving a Union flag – I doubt whether I will ever wave one again – not singing hymns, saying prayers or protesting, but like a dog and asked the government to put in my hand the document that sold my birthright." After the initial shock had worn off, mass Unionist protest spread across Northern Ireland. On the Loyalist community, however, the Agreement also had another effect. It set in motion the search for alternatives, one of which was the 1987 "Commonsense" proposal by the UDA's thinktank, the Ulster Political Research Group.

At the same time, Loyalist paramilitaries saw the Anglo-Irish Agreement as proof that the British government was caving in to Republican violence. This perception was further underlined when Republican violence rose significantly in 1986 following a substantial arms shipment from Libya. The IRA had now acquired sufficient weapons for the "final push" and Loyalists believed that the only way to counter this was by increasing their own level of threat. Consequently, the number of deaths was on the increase again, rising from 61 in 1986 to 93 in 1987. Shootings rose from 392 in 1986 to 674 in 1987. And the number of bombs planted increased from 254 in 1986 to 384 in 1987.

The trail of destruction left by inter-communal violence was rivaled by an equally devastating economic downturn. From the early 1980s onwards, the manufacturing sector in Northern Ireland had started to decline again. International investment had been frightened off by the hunger strikes and a leap in oil prices plunged the province into recession. Manufacturing employment fell by a third between 1979 and 1986; 21.1 percent of the population were classed as out of work.

Poverty in Loyalist and Republican working-class areas remained a persistent problem. Despite government subventions, Northern Ireland headed the list of deprived regions in the United Kingdom. And when the 1989 Social Security Act introduced more rigid tests for employment availability, the gap between the rich and poor widened further. The continued social and political marginalization of the Loyalist community provided the perfect breeding ground for a younger and more radical generation to join the ranks of the paramilitaries.

In the late 1980s and early 1990s a number of factors came together and finally pushed Loyalism from reactiveness to proactiveness. Attempts to find a political solution were abruptly ended when the UDA's key political strategist, John McMichael, was killed by an IRA under-car booby-trap bomb on December 22, 1987. Soon after, on March 11, 1988, UDA chairman Andy Tyrie, who along with McMichael had been a restraining influence, resigned. The path was now wide open for the militants. This development was further compounded when, on September 14, 1989, Cambridgeshire Deputy Chief Constable John Stevens was appointed to investigate the possible collusion between British security forces and Loyalist paramilitaries. The investigation led to the arrest of a sizable number of senior UDA personnel, leaving the leadership to those who all along had pushed for a Loyalist offensive, along with the younger, more militant generation within the UDA. The final factor aiding the shift to a pro-active military strategy was the collapse of the Soviet Union and the consequent opening of Eastern Europe as a source of sophisticated, easily accessible, arms in large quantities. The combination of absence of restraining influences, the new militant leadership and the acquisition of high-tech weapons and explosives ensured that Loyalist violence, for the first time in the Troubles, surpassed Republican violence.

This context of radicalization, however, also gave rise to a new generation of Loyalist politicians, including Gary McMichael, who started to look for a political rather than military solution to the conflict. Relentless efforts behind the scenes resulted in the 1991 unilateral ceasefire, which was aimed at providing the so-called constitutional parties – the UUP, SDLP, DUP and Alliance – with a chance to come up with an agreement during the Brooke Talks. Unionist politicians, however, were as unsatisfactory a representation as ever from a Loyalist perspective and under the Unionist–Nationalist deadlock, the talks collapsed. The ceasefire broke down almost immediately and the conflict in Northern Ireland plunged into a renewed cycle of violence. The failure of the Brooke Talks focused Loyalist strategy, making it clear that the Ulster Democratic Party and Progressive Unionist Party had to be involved in future negotiations if these were to be successful. It also drove home the message that Loyalist paramilitaries and parties had to work together for a united Loyalist voice.

In 1993, after the breakdown of the Mayhew Talks, the Loyalist parties started playing a more active role in bringing about a shift to negotiation. The UDP urged the Combined Loyalist Military Command (CLMC) to set up a group to analyze the political situation and make recommendations, resulting in the establishment of the Loyalist Political Alliance. A number of other political developments had also been set in motion. The SDLP leader John Hume had embarked upon a dialogue with Sinn Féin President Gerry Adams as well as the Irish government. British Prime Minister John Major and Irish Taoiseach Albert Reynolds were also searching for a way to revive negotiations, resulting in the 1993 Downing Street Declaration. And, finally, Dublin had put out feelers toward the Loyalists.

In 1994, the CLMC started exploring the possibility of another ceasefire because the Downing Street Declaration had provided a new opportunity for talks and forced the IRA to lay its position on the table. There were intense discussions surrounding Loyalist strategy as a result of the emerging Nationalist position and great efforts were made to move the entire situation in a meaningful direction, especially as the war on the streets had reached an almost unprecedented degree of destruction. Ultimately, however, it was exactly this violence which empowered the Loyalist paramilitaries. They could now call a ceasefire and their political representatives could claim a seat at the negotiating table. They believed that they had put the IRA on the run; they had hit Republicanism where it hurt. They had shown the traditional Unionist leaders that they would no longer be marginalized, used, abused, and ignored. And, finally, they had suffered too long from inter-communal conflict to waste another opportunity for peace.

Part One–A Personal Perspective

Starting Off

1985 was a watershed in Ulster's history. It was the year the British and Irish governments imposed the Anglo-Irish Agreement, catapulting Northern Ireland into a period of severe political turmoil. It was also the time when I remember first becoming actively involved in political events. I was sixteen at the time and had just left school. Despite having managed to attain seven out of the eight qualifications I had sat, I declined an offer to carry on up the next rung of the educational ladder in favor of getting out there into the real world to make a living. This is something I now regret from time to time.

I was always aware of political events, which I suppose is not surprising since my father was such a prominent political activist. I was a Loyalist and held a strong sense of identity but had not considered taking any active role in expressing that Loyalism politically or otherwise until 1985. Having left school, I found myself in the middle of the events that engulfed my country within a few short months.

Margaret Thatcher, my Prime Minister, and Garret FitzGerald, the Irish Taoiseach, formally signed the Anglo-Irish Agreement on November 15 in Hillsborough Castle, which is set in the small picturesque village of Hillsborough, just a couple of miles up the road from where I lived. I had just started my first job which was in the local unemployment office. I had gone along to register as seeking employment like all school leavers and a few weeks later they had given me a job writing unemployment cheques.

The "Agreement" as it became known, enflamed the emotions of the entire Unionist community, fusing all shades of Unionism and Loyalism together in opposition to it. It was seen as a betrayal, negotiated over the heads of the people of Northern Ireland and implemented against their will. The Nationalist SDLP had been involved in the process which delivered the Agreement while Unionism had been excluded. Indeed, the process was so secretive and exclusive that only a few members of the British cabinet were aware of the detail.

The reasons for such secrecy became obvious immediately. The Agreement effectively gave the government of the Irish Republic a structural role in the affairs of Northern Ireland. This was an extraordinary step, taken unilaterally by both governments without the consent of the people of Northern Ireland and without consulting them. The strength of opposition that resulted must have been predictable but, despite that, the Agreement was forced upon the people. It was clear that both governments were prepared to follow through their plans to impose their will, regardless of the views of those it affected.

Opposition to it was not just confined to the Unionist people in Ulster. Ian Gow who was then British Treasury Minister and who was a close friend of Margaret Thatcher resigned, saying that the Agreement would only "prolong, and not diminish Ulster's agony." The IRA murdered Gow not long afterwards. Mary Robinson, later to become the President of Ireland, resigned from the Irish Labor Party, saying "I do not believe it can achieve its objective of securing peace and stability within Northern Ireland or on the island as a whole."

As my work colleagues and I were civil servants, working in a government building, we were not supposed to have a view on political matters, and discussion of such things was actively discouraged. But, following the Agreement, I found it easy to distinguish who was what in our office. Feelings were so strong at that time that you could sense the divisions opening up among the staff. I don't recall any particular instance where there was any overt display of hostility or argument but the tension was there, bubbling under the surface, nonetheless.

Unionist opposition to the Agreement included a campaign of civil disobedience and protests in a variety of forms. I felt compelled to become involved in this campaign and took part in many of the protests that were being organized, while keeping my views firmly to myself at work. I did not know whether anyone had realized who my father was or made the connection, but I was not going to go out of my way to draw unnecessary attention to myself. However, on a couple of occasions, I did expose my sympathies. It was very naïve of me to think I could depend on any degree of real anonymity. People knew all right and it prejudiced them toward me either positively or negatively, but I was too young to read the signs.

One of the most popular forms of protest was for people willfully to withhold their property rates. The idea was that, if people did so in sufficient numbers, the system would become overloaded as it tried to pursue offenders. One day, a group of protesters marched into the Rates Collection Office in Lisburn, which happened to be situated on the floor above ours. They promptly locked themselves in and forced the office to stop business. I heard about this and sneaked upstairs to where they were. Curiously, there was no one standing about in the corridor. I was surprised because I would have thought this phenomenon would have attracted a lot of interest, at least from the rest of the staff working in the building who would, no doubt, have found it an interesting distraction on an otherwise dull day. It turned out that the area had been put off limits while it was decided what to do about the protesters.

It seemed a bit of a waste of energy that this protest was taking place and probably no one apart from those inside the building knew of it. So I went outside to the closest public telephone and rang the BBC and Ulster Television, informing them of the unfolding protest. I then went back up to the Rates Office and slid a note under the barricaded doors informing the protesters that news teams would be there within half an hour to cover the event. I slipped back into my office and went back to work, happy that I had helped the campaign against the Agreement in some small way, yet also realizing that this could have cost me my job. But it seemed the right thing to do.

On another occasion, I sailed a bit closer to the wind. On March 3, 1986 a general strike took place. It became known as the "day of action." Across Northern Ireland those who were opposed to the Anglo-Irish Agreement did not turn up for work and took part in public protests instead. The country largely came to a standstill for twenty-four hours. I took part in a protest across a bridge that crossed the River Lagan giving access to Lisburn town center. Civil servants naturally were not allowed to take part in any such action and were threatened with dismissal. I remember one of my supervisors walked over the bridge, attempting to get to work in spite of the protests. He looked over and I am sure he recognized me. When I went to work the next day, I was called into a private office and asked to make a statement explaining why I had failed to report for work. I told them with a grin that I could not get past the roadblocks. Nothing came of it. I suppose that so many people had come out in support of the campaign that it was not practical for action to be taken against them.

A steady barrage of protest had been taking place since November 1985 and the pressure was being kept up with examples of resistance on a daily basis right across Northern Ireland. Just a week after the Agreement was signed, more than 200,000 people had marched on Belfast City Hall to show their opposition. I was one of them and remember this as being the rallying call that had prompted the organization of structured resistance in local areas. Mass mobilization and civil disobedience was considered the best way to demonstrate physically the strength of opposition in the Unionist community and to place sufficient strain on the government's resources to force it to take notice of public opinion. The views of the people had not been sought when the government had imposed the Agreement, and the objective was to show it that it could not rule without consent. Thatcher had consistently ignored calls for a referendum. So, in order to force a test of the democratic wishes of the people, fifteen of the seventeen Members of Parliament for Northern Ireland resigned their seats, forcing by-elections. I myself was not old enough to vote, but I expressed my opposition in other ways.

I became active in the Ulster Clubs, which was an organization formed just before the Agreement was signed, with the objective of opposing the Anglo-Irish initiative by bringing together Unionists and Loyalists from all kinds of backgrounds. It was a collaborative initiative between my father and Allen

Wright, a Loyalist from Portadown. Clubs were set up all across Northern Ireland. I joined the Lisburn Club along with members of the DUP, UUP, Orange Order, Ulster Resistance, and UDA, as well as clergy and community activists. This movement was intended to be the broadest of churches and allow all shades of the Unionist spectrum to be part of it to express our shared objections to the Agreement without any conflict which might otherwise arise out of ideological differences.

David Trimble was chairman of the Lisburn Club for a time, as was I. One of our local objectives was to devise an emergency plan for the area in the event of a breakdown of law and order. Similar plans had been fashioned in 1974 for the period of the UWC strike allowing local communities to function and sustain themselves. This time there was a different rationale to the exercise. This was preparation for the possibility that, if the government consistently failed to recognize the expressed will of the majority of people in Northern Ireland, a point would come when the people would be forced to seize control. That was one of the contingencies we were encouraged to consider seriously.

Another form of protest was an anti-Agreement walk, in which people walked from Londonderry to Belfast over the course of a week, stopping in towns and villages to rally support. By the time it reached Belfast, the crowd numbered tens of thousands. My father took part in the entire walk, traveling during the day and sleeping in local church halls at night as the protesters crossed Northern Ireland. I remember he complained that Ian Paisley only turned up as they would come to the limits of towns; he would get out of his car, walk through the town centers, and jump back in his car again when they got to the other side. I took part in the last two legs of the march and I remember chatting to a guy who was involved in a parachute club. He talked me and a few others into doing a charity parachute jump. You had to raise sponsorship for the jump, part of which would pay for the plane ride and the rest would go to charity. My Dad thought it was a great idea, but then he wasn't going to be doing it. I raised a fair amount of money and went to the club, spent a day training for the jump, and wondered why I had let myself be talked into jumping out of a perfectly good airplane. In the end, the weather did not permit us to do the jump and we were sent home, which suited me just fine, especially as the money still went to charity and I didn't have to stake my life on a bit of silk. So everyone was happy.

Another major rally was organized to coincide with the first anniversary of the signing of the Agreement in November 1986. Around 200,000 people gathered once again at Belfast City Hall. The slogan which for the previous year had been "Ulster Says No!" was re-marketed as "Ulster *Still* Says No!" It was becoming clear that, despite the successful mobilization of opposition and ongoing protest, little political progress was being made. The rhetoric from James Molyneaux and Ian Paisley, who had formed an anti-Agreement alliance over the course of the past year, was becoming worn. The Anglo-Irish Agreement had not been scrapped and it was evident that no coherent political alternative had been devised by the Unionist "leadership." I did not know this at the time but it had been obvious to some Loyalists that, behind the united front projected by Molyneaux and Paisley, no serious alternative was being proposed. Ulster saying "No!" to the Agreement was not in itself going to remove it, and, since it was also an international treaty, Thatcher was not going to back down in the absence of a sensible alternative to replace it. As a result, the UDA, under the guidance of my father, started working on a document designed to encourage debate on a political alternative.

The fusion of Unionism against the Agreement had facilitated a degree of cooperation and collaboration between the different factions of Unionism and Loyalism rarely seen before, and did so effectively. This level of camaraderie across the spectrum of Unionism was never to be witnessed again. As was the case in 1974, the grassroots acted as one in response to the perceived crisis but, as had been the case back then, faith was placed in the ability of political Unionism to give pro-active leadership. By the end of 1986, a year on from the Agreement, the anticipated deliverance from the crisis had not come, and there was no apparent strategy in place. People power and civil disobedience was an important and necessary part of a successful strategy but it was only a part. It had to be a marriage of physical pressure and political innovation. That, unfortunately, was absent.

Meanwhile, physical conflict was escalating. Margaret Thatcher had described the Anglo-Irish Agreement as an instrument that would bring "better security." What it had, however, delivered to the people of Northern Ireland was a renewal of the conflict, a resurgence of Loyalist violence, a breakdown of community relations, an alienation of the Unionist community, and a crippled relationship between Unionism and the British government. Since 1985, every British government policy decision on Northern Ireland has been viewed with suspicion. The Anglo-Irish process has been viewed by Unionism as a gradual erosion of democratic rights, following an agenda that was being driven firmly in the direction of greater dilution of Northern Ireland's sovereignty within the United Kingdom. This is one of the reasons why Unionism did not grasp the peace process as readily as Nationalism did in the 1990s.

In 1986, 61 people were killed in the Troubles. There were 392 shootings and 254 bombs planted, each statistic an increase on 1985. In fact, Loyalist violence had almost come to a standstill by 1985 but began to increase following the signing of the Agreement. Yet, the IRA was still responsible for the vast majority of violence during this period. In July 1986, the Republican paramilitary leadership said that any civilian working for the security forces would now be considered to be a "collaborator" and executed. The list of those whom the IRA decided were "legitimate targets" included anyone supplying fuel, cleaning services or food to the police or army. It also included firms that supplied vending machines to police stations. And, not surprisingly, Sinn Féin fully backed the IRA statement. Two days later, the IRA enforced its new policy statement by murdering a Protestant businessman.

It was apparent that the IRA had deliberately cast a net that was so wide it covered just about anyone and lent a contrived legitimacy to its desire to murder Protestants. A week later, the IRA shot dead a Protestant electrician, justifying his assassination on the grounds that he had carried out electrical repairs at a local Ulster Defense Regiment base. The Provos had given their sectarian campaign carte blanche and, as a result, pressure was mounting on Loyalists to widen their campaign in response. I remember having almost a sense of panic during this period. Things were very grim indeed. It seemed that the conflict was taking on a momentum that had the potential to spiral out of control. Taken against the backdrop of the political tension surrounding the Anglo-Irish Agreement there was real chance of a complete breakdown of society. I was to know that feeling more than once, as in later years, at times, it looked like we were racing toward civil war. The UDA had created a new organization called the Ulster Defense Force, its function being to train young men and women in survival and military tactics. The purpose of this group can only have been to defend Unionist areas in the event of total war. The existence of the UDF was publicized and knowledge of its formation served to heighten the sense that society was preparing for the worst. Toward the end of the year, the atmosphere was becoming more highly charged. Colonel Gadaffi, who had become the IRA's main arms supplier, called in an interview on Irish television for "all Irish youth in the North and South to participate in the struggle for the liberation of Ulster."

Commonsense – A Way Forward

My father once described Northern Ireland as being "on a motorway toward confrontation." This was in January 1987 as the Ulster Political Research Group, the UDA's political think tank, published its "Commonsense" document. It constituted the first considered political proposals to emerge from Unionism in response to the Anglo-Irish Agreement. The document received a broad welcome but, at the same time, it was dismissed by the mainstream Unionist parties who perceived it to be an embarrassing exposure of their lack of activity. Molyneaux and Paisley had developed no political alternative to the Agreement, while the "Commonsense" proposals were a challenge from grassroots Loyalism. In fact, worse than that, it came from militant Loyalism which the Unionist leadership preferred to be the muscle and not the brains of the operation.

"Commonsense" advocated the creation of a Northern Ireland government, devolved from the British Parliament. It proposed that the new arrangements should recognize the need for the two communities in Northern Ireland to co-determine their future together, and it outlined a model for proportionality and shared responsibility in the new government. It advocated protective mechanisms to safeguard the rights of the people, in the form of a written constitution and a Northern Ireland bill of rights. The premise of the document was that an alternative path forward had to be found if we were to avoid civil war. The Anglo-Irish Agreement was not a device that could deliver progress because it could not command the support of more than ten percent of the people. The lesson to be learnt from the Agreement was that a political solution cannot be imposed, nor can any initiative succeed unless it commands broad cross-community support.

My father was a dedicated Loyalist and strongly believed that the UDA had a role to perform in the defense of the Unionist community from armed Republican aggression and political coercion, even if that meant doing so as a combatant in the conflict. But he also believed that war, while a reality of our division, was avoidable. The conflict had become embedded over such a long period that it had become an apparition of normality. "This is just the way things are and we should accept that," seemed to be the mentality that had taken hold. The conflict was infinitely sustainable and it was being demonstrated that it could easily increase in momentum and viciousness, but where was that leading? He argued that those who were most closely involved in the conflict could have the greatest capacity to look beyond it and could find a way forward because of their understanding of the consequences of war.

Molyneaux and Paisley were not offering any serious political proposals for such a way forward, and, in the meantime, the conflict was escalating. It was not going to be those in the leadership of the Unionist parties that had to fight the war. Rather it was the ordinary people in the grassroots areas who were bearing the brunt of the conflict. Thus the war had to be brought to an end because, if it was not, it would turn into conflict for its own sake and would only end through the domination of one community over the other through violence. Since 1969, the IRA had failed to force Northern Ireland out of the United Kingdom, or its Unionist population into submission. But military resistance against Republicans equally had not succeeded in eradicating the IRA. So a quick end to the conflict was not in sight. Therefore, the UDA believed that it had to take the initiative by proposing that a stable future could only be built if there was a political initiative that commanded wide-spread support. To achieve that, however, it also had to recognize that there were political limits beyond which each community would not go. In essence, what was proposed was a structure for government that allowed all sections to play a full and equal role in society within a framework of government where both Nationalists and Unionists had to guarantee each other's future, rather than engaging in a political tug of war.

The proposals were innovative and took many commentators by surprise. As the Ulster Defense Association is the largest of the paramilitary organizations, it holds its share of responsibility for the political violence that had taken place over the previous decade and a half. Consequently, some people were skeptical of the progressive character of the "Commonsense" proposals. The kind of model being suggested had not been put forward before and was perhaps a little ahead of its time. It is interesting that most of the Northern Ireland political parties adopted similar models in later years and the form of government agreed for Northern Ireland in the 1998 Stormont Agreement is not dissimilar to that outlined in 1987.

While "Commonsense" was not embraced by the UUP and DUP, it did, however, provoke some activity. Less than a month later, they set up a "task force" to examine possible alternatives to the Anglo-Irish Agreement. Frank Millar, UUP Honorary Secretary, and DUP Deputy Leader, Peter Robinson, headed it. They reported to Paisley and Molyneaux on July 2, 1987, proposing a form of devolved power-sharing administration in Northern Ireland. Their leaders effectively ignored the report and, as a result, Millar resigned from the Unionist Party. He is now the Westminster correspondent for the *Irish Times*. Robinson also resigned his deputy leadership but later took up that office once again. It had been firmly exposed that the Unionist leadership was not prepared to enter a debate on alternatives to the Agreement and that the task force had merely been a smoke-screen for their inaction.

The dangerous direction of the conflict was further reinforced by the Enniskillen Bomb later that year. On November 8, the IRA planted a huge bomb at the cenotaph in Enniskillen, County Fermanagh, as people gathered to remember the dead of the two world wars. Eleven civilians were murdered in the blast that sent shock waves around the world and it became known as the Poppy Day Massacre. I watched the news coverage on television that Sunday and, seeing them pull people from the rubble, wondered how much worse could it get? It angered and repulsed me but I could not empathize with the grief that such atrocities bring. That, however, changed soon.

On December 22, 1987, I went to a concert in the Ulster Hall in Belfast with my then girlfriend, Elaine, and a number of other friends. About an hour into the concert, the singer of the band made an announcement. He said, "If there's a Gary McMichael in the hall, would he please go to the front entrance. It's very important." I waded through the throng of people toward the entrance, to find Elaine had made it there before me, and there was a man I recognized from Lisburn standing waiting, obviously feeling very uncomfortable. Before he had a chance to speak, I asked him, "Is he dead?" He replied, "I'm not telling you. Your mum is outside. She'll talk to you." My mother was in the street standing beside Elaine's parents' car, who had brought her down. She put her arms around me and told me, "Your daddy's been killed." I had known anyhow. As soon as my name was called out in the hall, I knew.

My father had left his home on an errand to take turkeys around to the wives of some of the political prisoners from Lisburn. It was Christmas and, traditionally, the prisoners' families were helped out in some small way. My dad did not have to deliver them personally but he chose to do so. He was going to bring my brother Saul along with him but decided not to. He was rushing because he was late, due to having mislaid the car keys. When he climbed into his car, the motion threw a mercury tilt switch which detonated a bomb that had been magnetically attached to the underside of his car, just under the driver's seat. That was at 8:05 p.m. The explosion was heard for miles around, and the barman on duty that night in my father's public house in Lisburn center told me afterwards that the telephone immediately began ringing as people phoned thinking the bomb had been there. My father was dead on arrival at the hospital. He was thirty-nine years old.

The next few days are a bit of a blur now, but I remember the huge numbers of people who came to my grandparents' house, where his body had been brought, as well as the hundreds upon hundreds of cards and flowers and telephone calls. As the oldest son, I took a lot of the weight of the organization of the funeral, along with my uncle, Thomas. We went to the funeral directors to make the necessary arrangements, placed the death notices and met the people who came to sympathize at the house. These are customary responsibilities for such things. Less customary were the visits to the police station to coordinate the funeral. The RUC was anxious about the possibility of a paramilitary display at the funeral, and we were worried about security to protect the funeral from attack. A number of incidents had occurred around my grandparents' house which raised concern. One time, a taxi from a staunch Republican area was spotted cruising past the house, raising fears that the IRA was scouting out the locality. We were also concerned about an over-reaction from the police. Earlier that year, the funeral of an IRA man had been postponed twice and took three days finally to take place after confrontation between mourners and the police. I was not going to have that happen with my father's funeral. He would be laid to rest with the dignity he deserved.

Traditionally, funerals in Northern Ireland take place on the third day after the death. That was not possible in this case because that was Christmas Day, so my father was buried on Boxing Day. The procession numbered almost ten thousand and walked along a five-mile route from my grandparents' home to the church and then through Lisburn town center, stopping briefly outside his business before proceeding to the graveyard. At one point, the funeral was forced to stop because the RUC over-reacted. The coffin was draped with a UDA flag and an Ulster flag. Six men on each side wearing white shirts, black ties and black armbands flanked it. A lone piper led the procession. This was the format for the funeral agreed with the police, but a senior officer drafted in to oversee the occasion decided that the dress adorning the men who flanked the coffin looked too much like a uniform and sent RUC officers in to flank these gentlemen. In turn, mourners moved to flank the policemen. We stopped the cortège and Andy Tyrie, the head of the UDA and a life-long colleague of my father, told the police that, if they did not move their men, then the funeral cortège was staying put. Thankfully, they saw sense and we were able to continue. I was very angry at the time and the local police superintendent came to apologize afterwards. I have no doubt that he would not have been as callous as his superior.

No one has ever faced trial for my father's murder and probably never will. I know the truth. I know the names, but they have not been brought to justice. My life changed irreversibly from that point, naturally. The Poppy Day Massacre had been less than two months before and one of the memorable features in the aftermath of that terrible event was the words of forgiveness, freely given by the late Gordon Wilson, whose daughter Marie was murdered in that explosion. I have never been able to understand how people found themselves able to forgive in the midst of the grief they were suffering. I have never considered forgiving those who murdered my father. They destroyed my life and I hate them for it as much today as I did back then. But I have learnt to temper my feelings and channel them in a direction which, I hope, has produced a positive energy rather than a destructive one.

I often look back and consider what might have been if my father were still alive and free to take us on the journey he had just begun. It would be interesting to know where that would have led. I would almost certainly not have followed my father into politics. When I was at school, my dad had bought me a personal computer when they had only just come onto the market and, while the technology was extremely rudimentary, I took a great fascination in it. I was not permitted to select computer studies as an O-level subject because I was not in a sufficiently advanced math class. It seemed I was not smart enough to study computing despite the fact that I was constructing programs on my own machine. This truncation of my aspiration was one of the reasons I chose not to carry on my education. I felt bitter that I was not allowed to pursue the educational avenue that interested me. Upon leaving school, I went to night classes and acquired my computer qualifications there. I seriously hoped to work myself up to a point where I could step into the computer industry to develop a career. At the time of my father's death, I was in the middle of an advanced computing course at Belfast College for Further Education, but dropped out after his murder.

I had resigned from the civil service a couple of months earlier to commit myself on a full-time basis to a community project. My involvement in the Ulster Clubs had introduced me to a number of people who were interested in taking a more active role in addressing social disadvantage in working-class areas. Together we formed a community organization in Hillhall, one of the working-class housing estates in Lisburn. We had no experience in community development but successfully got the project off the ground with minimal resources.

As is the case in many such areas, Hillhall had a serious unemployment problem, and there were neither recreational facilities nor any activity groups in the area. Kids hung around street corners, bored and unruly, adding to the social problems in the estate. Housing conditions were appalling and the Housing Authority found it difficult to find decent tenants because of the problems in the area and the poor standards of their own property. There was a very low level of esteem and the whole community was on a downward spiral. No one was trying to help them and the knowledge or confidence was not there for the community to help itself. We started a residents' committee to try to tackle some of these issues. As I was the only one who did not come from the area, and because I had still not turned eighteen at that stage, I probably had a bit of a credibility problem. However, I think I proved myself quickly and soon became a principal activist in the group.

We had nowhere to meet so our gatherings took place in each other's houses. After a few months we persuaded the Northern Ireland Housing Executive to donate one of its properties, a three-bedroom house, to us and we set up an office there to provide advice and help to the people of the estate. We had limited resources but raised some money through local businesses and purchased a pool table and a dartboard. Suddenly, the kids had a place to go at night and, while it was tiny, it still provided a place for them to get out of the cold. Unfortunately, it did not sustain itself and, a couple of years later, it ran into the ground due to a lack of financial support and a shortage of committed activists necessary to overcome the financial weaknesses.

My own interest in and commitment to the community group had also changed with my father's death. The things that had been important to me up to that point had lost in significance. I cannot explain why my attitude changed in reaction to his death, but it did. So I began looking for something else to do.

The Establishment of the UDP

In June 1988, I took a temporary job with Farset Youth and Community Development Ltd on the Springfield Road in Belfast. It was the largest community project in Northern Ireland and situated on the peaceline between Protestant and Catholic West Belfast, drawing unemployed people from both sides of the community together to work with each other. I was placed on the Somme project, which was one of the many projects Farset had devised. Its purpose was to enhance understanding of the role that the people of Northern Ireland had played in the First World War, in particular at the Battle of the Somme. It was a fascinating project and I learnt a lot there.

Around that time, I was coming into contact with other people who expressed to me their deep regret that my father's death seemed to have extinguished the political dynamic within Loyalism. I do not remember specifically how but, over a period of a few months, a number of such people had gravitated toward each other in order to find a way to keep alive the principles outlined by "Commonsense." We wanted to carry forward my father's vision and offer leadership to the working-class Loyalist community. It was clear that, at all levels, there was an unsatisfactory representation of the needs of Loyalists, both at the macro-political and the socio-economic levels. So we decided to reform the Ulster Loyalist Democratic Party (ULDP), first launched by my father in June 1981. Then it had been a device created by the UDA to provide Loyalist political expression and was in a way a reaction to Sinn Féin's re-emergence as a political force during the H-Block campaign and the hunger strikes. The ULDP was to be a Loyalist political voice to counter Republicanism. The fact that the UDA had created the ULDP merely as an extension of itself, however, had not made it attractive to the electorate. Consequently, the party never really took off.

So, in 1988, we reformed the ULDP as an independent political party. Naturally, some of the activists were former or current members of the UDA, but the objective was to create a political movement that was open and attractive to any person who supported our policies and aims. The UDA was not a proscribed organization at that point and it was supportive of our initiative, welcoming perhaps the fact that we had decided to establish a vehicle that could engender political interest within the Loyalist community and promote the ideals it had presented in the "Commonsense" document. When the Ulster Political Research Group had published its proposals it did so to provoke debate, not to prepare a political platform for the UDA. My father had said at the time that the intention was to throw "Commonsense" onto the table so that others could discuss it and perhaps it would contribute to the debate in a constructive way. The leadership of the Unionist parties had studiously ignored the proposals to the extent of rubbishing their own task force report, which had clearly taken a lot from "Commonsense." Therefore, there was no objection from the UDA to our willingness to pick up the document and run with it as the backbone of our political philosophy.

We formed an executive and agreed that, in order to win support and respect within our community, we had to prove our worth. Loyalism had been misrepresented and manipulated by the DUP and Ulster Unionists to such an extent that, at a local level, there was little faith in their elected representatives. The district councils were filled with useless individuals who did little on the ground to better the disadvantaged in their constituencies. That was something I had learned very quickly in my experience with the community group in Lisburn. It had been virtually impossible to get support from elected representatives for developments in working-class areas. These people did not have the interest of the people at heart and were not representing them. We, as the ULDP, had to convince the people that we would represent their interests and, by working with local communities on the ground, earn their trust and support. Only over time could we expect to break the traditional voting pattern that maintained the unsatisfactory status quo. Generations of traditional voting along sectarian lines resulted in an almost automatic response from the electorate. The logic of "My father voted for the Unionist Party, so I vote for the Unionist Party" had to be challenged. The DUP, which had established a strong base in the late sixties and early seventies, had been successful – now it was our turn. Nevertheless, it was very difficult to convince people to change their pattern of voting and this resulted in District Councils being full of eejits who had no idea of what was going on in their constituencies and were there because they were Unionist or Nationalist, not on the basis of their ability to represent the interests of the community. We had to break this mold and show the local community that we could make a difference.

We held a series of public meetings around the country which were well attended and, in the space of two months, eight constituency associations were formed. I recall convening a public meeting in Lisburn Orange Hall, which had attracted more than a hundred people. It was the first time I had to speak in public. Being only nineteen, I was very, very nervous. In fact, I had worked myself up into such a state that I made a real pig's ear out of my speech. I thought that I had single-handedly managed to wipe out the party in Lisburn before it had even been formed. Luckily, the people there excused my embarrassing performance and Lisburn became the strongest of our constituency associations. Most of those who had come along had done so out of respect for my father and that was an important factor in helping us to build a strong base in Lisburn.

As we were putting the ULDP together, the so-called constitutional parties – the UUP, DUP, SDLP and Alliance – started to explore the possibility of inter-party talks. On October 14, 1988, the four parties were flown to Duisburg, West Germany for two days of discussions. The neutral environment, however, did little to encourage progress. As the initiative was surrounded by suspicion, and the parties were unable to overcome their differences over the Anglo-Irish Agreement, little was achieved.

In May 1989, the ULDP participated in its first democratic elections. Despite having virtually no resources and only eight months to build a profile, we succeeded in getting our first local councilor, Ken Kerr, elected in Londonderry. As the election coordinator – not having run myself – I considered this to be a start. But, despite our electoral success, the situation of the party changed little. We still had no money and were operating out of a single room in the back of a Loyalist souvenir shop on the Newtownards Road in Belfast. I manned this makeshift office along with a lady from Glencairn in West Belfast. Our resources barely covered petrol and bus expenses for the two of us each week and our equipment consisted of a filing cabinet and a wonky typewriter that did not print evenly on the page. Yet we managed to create the illusion that the ULDP was a bigger organization than it really was, firing statements to the newspapers every single day on every issue imaginable. We bombarded the media with so much information and comments that they started to give us a fair run of coverage.

After a while, we managed to get some modest financial backing and opened offices in Lisburn and in Londonderry, equipped with antique computers and fax machines – a major step up compared to what we had survived on so far. With four years to go until the next local elections, we were able to work on building a stronger profile for the party in general and for individuals in local areas, myself included.

At the end of 1989, we decided that we would change the name of the party to Ulster Democratic Party, dropping the Loyalist. This was a matter of strong debate among us and some were opposed to the change, but the decision was taken in order to try to make the party more attractive to a broader public. Since our launch in 1988, the media had continued to refer to us as the UDA's political wing. This was factually untrue, but the result was that it stigmatized the party and was making it difficult for sections of society to embrace our views. There was a line of thought that, while we were principally active in working-class areas, our policies should be actively promoted across all sections of the community. The truth was that many people did not look past our name long enough to read our policies. Anyway, in retrospect, I think this was a mistake, a case of trying to be all things to all people and forgetting that one must learn to crawl before trying to run.

While IRA violence usually subsided in the week following Christmas, one could be certain that gunfire or an explosion would follow the church bells that chimed in the New Year reasonably quickly. The first victim of the IRA in the new year was one of our members, Harry Dickey. Harry was a taxi-driver with family, who lived and worked in East Belfast. He was murdered on January 2, 1990 when an under-car booby-trap bomb, identical to that which killed my father, exploded under his taxi outside his home.

There was no justification for Harry Dickey's murder for he was just a family man trying to earn a living who happened to be a member of the UDP. As we learnt to our cost, the IRA was very willing and prepared to attack and kill our party members. It was just another part of its program of genocide. Harry was killed because he was a Protestant. His killers did not need another reason. The IRA has been falsely labeled as some form of highly principled and dedicated guerrilla force, driven by Republican objectives of uniting Protestant, Catholic and Dissenter. The truth is that the IRA is deeply sectarian in its character and while the main thrust of its terror campaign has concentrated on members of the British Army and the RUC, it has consistently pursued the extermination of Protestants.

Indeed, in areas along the border between Northern Ireland and the Republic of Ireland, there has been a campaign that amounts to ethnic cleansing. Over the course of the Troubles, Republicans have viciously murdered the male family members of small Protestant communities in isolated rural areas in an attempt to drive Protestant families from their homes and their land, so that it may be then occupied by Catholics. In pursuit of that objective, Republicans broadened the remit of their classification of legitimate targets to cast the widest possible net to justify their sectarianism and carried out acts of barbaric mass murder over the years. For instance, on January 5, 1976, Republicans stopped a workman's van in Kingsmills, separated the Catholic driver from his ten Protestant passengers, then lined up the Protestants and machine-gunned them to death. Another example is Darkley, County Armagh, where, on November 20, 1983, Republican gunmen entered a church hall and shot dead three church elders, wounding seven others. These were acts of pure hatred that instilled fear within the Protestant community, causing many to flee.

The Brooke Talks and the First Loyalist Ceasefire

The Secretary of State for Northern Ireland from 1989 to 1992 was Sir Peter Brooke. He earned the somewhat unfortunate nickname "babbling Brooke" because of his propensity to mumble his way through conversations and tie himself in knots when giving media interviews. He gave his name to the Brooke Talks that took place in 1991, consisting of discussions between the four largest political parties in Northern Ireland at the time: the UUP, SDLP, DUP and the Alliance Party. It had taken months for these parties to agree to enter talks with each other in order to develop a political blueprint for Northern Ireland. There was suspicion on all sides as a result of the previous experience of failed initiatives as well as the concern that the agenda was being set by the British and Irish governments to the disadvantage of Unionism. In 1990, Brooke had made a significant policy statement in which he announced that the British government had "no selfish strategic or economic interest in Northern Ireland." Essentially, this was interpreted by Unionists to mean that their government in Westminster no longer desired to have Northern Ireland remain a member of the United Kingdom, despite it being the democratic wish of the majority of its inhabitants. It was another concession to Nationalism designed to assure that the British government was neutral on the future of Northern Ireland. This was very disturbing for Unionists for, while their government was pronouncing its neutrality, the government of the Republic of Ireland held a very clear and public agenda to pursue the reunification of Ireland, thus creating a definite power imbalance.

Unionists saw the proposed talks as a vehicle for the British and Irish governments to build on the Anglo-Irish Agreement, which was an unacceptable proposition. Subsequently, a commitment was given that the objective of the talks would be to agree "a more broadly based agreement" than the 1985 treaty. The SDLP saw little advantage in engaging in talks because it believed that, since the 1985 agreement had been constructed without Unionist input, the only possible outcome of cross-community talks would be a weakening of the Nationalist ethos put in place five years earlier.

Despite misgivings, the parties finally agreed to discuss political matters in a three-stranded format. The three strands of negotiation were to deal with the relationships within Northern Ireland, the relationships between Northern Ireland and the Republic of Ireland, and those between the United Kingdom and the Republic of Ireland. Additionally, the process would be subject to the premise that nothing would be agreed until everything was agreed. This provided a safety net for all parties in the sense that no single element of the negotiations could be viewed in isolation but had to be considered as part of a package. This was viewed with some suspicion at the time but proved a central principle to the achievement of agreement in the successful 1996–98 negotiations.

Loyalists were not represented at the Brooke Talks and were not consulted by the British government at the time. Yet, despite the exclusionist nature of the talks process, Loyalists were enthusiastic to see political progress occur. In order to support the opportunity that the initiative presented, the main Loyalist paramilitary groupings, the Ulster Freedom Fighters (UFF), Ulster Defense Association (UDA), Ulster Volunteer Force (UVF) and Red Hand Commando (RHC) called a ceasefire under the guise of the Combined Loyalist Military Command (CLMC). Their ceasefire was designed to allow the political parties involved the potential to negotiate in a non-violent environment. It was also crucially an indication from paramilitary forces that there was room for an end to conflict if there was satisfactory political progress.

The Ulster Democratic Party was centrally involved in negotiating this cessation and persuading the Loyalist armed groups to end hostilities for the duration of the talks. The ceasefire was announced on April 17, 1991 and was to come into force on April 30, to coincide with the beginning of the talks. Ray Smallwoods was the principle liaison between the UDP and the paramilitary groups at this point. David Adams and I were involved also, but to a lesser extent. Ray had been a dedicated Loyalist all his life and became involved in the party after his release from the Maze prison, where he had been a political prisoner for eight years. He was a close friend of my father and believed wholeheartedly in his vision of a political resolution of the conflict. His strength and determination over this period were singularly important to the courageous initiative taken by the Loyalist armed groups in 1991.

Unfortunately, however, violence still continued in Northern Ireland and beyond as the IRA intensified its campaign. The challenge of suspending conflict while peace talks took place was rejected by Republicans and the Provos escalated their activity deliberately to provoke a breakdown of the Loyalist ceasefire and the collapse of the political talks. Massive car-bombs were planted in Protestant housing estates, aimed at causing the greatest possible destruction and death.

A leading member of the Orange Order was murdered by the IRA as part of its sectarian campaign in the hope that further pressure would be placed on the Loyalist ceasefire. In another push, on June 29, the IRA resorted to striking once again at the UDP. Cecil McKnight was our North West Chairman and had been a candidate in the 1989 elections. He was shot dead by two IRA gunmen as he was in the living-room of his home in Londonderry. It was somewhat ironic that, at the moment he was murdered, he was discussing his personal security with two RUC officers who had called to warn him of a threat to his life. The local RUC base was merely one hundred meters from his home and the IRA murder squad ran past it to get away from the scene.

Four days later, on July 3, the Brooke Talks collapsed and, with them, the Loyalist ceasefire. Negotiations had barely reached the point of discussing serious political issues. Most of the time had been taken up by wrangles over chairmanships of the strands as well as venues and agendas. One of the most serious obstacles to their success was the insistence by the governments that there should be a fixed time-frame of ten weeks for the duration of the negotiations. As a condition for the initiation of the process, it had been agreed that the meetings of the Anglo-Irish Intergovernmental Conference, which was the engine of the Anglo-Irish Agreement, would be suspended for that period. Despite the lack of progress, the governments refused to abandon the next scheduled meeting of the Conference and, therefore, forced the talks to a close.

The reaction within Loyalism was disquieting. While blame was thrown from and at all sides, Loyalists gauged the collapse of the talks to be a collective failure of everyone involved. We had been working for years to encourage the paramilitary groups that there had to be a political alternative to violence but, having taken the initiative in good faith to enhance the opportunity for political dialogue, they believed they had given faith too blindly. The result of their contribution to the process had been an escalation in Republican violence and a failure by the political forces to engage seriously in the negotiations. Two fundamental lessons were learned from this experience. Firstly, Loyalists could not be sure that there was any genuine interest on the part of the IRA to move beyond the conflict. Secondly, never again would they allow Loyalism to be represented by proxy by the traditional Unionist parties while legitimate Loyalist political voices were excluded.

The influence that the UDP had worked to build up with the paramilitary groups was badly affected by the breakdown of the talks. We found it more difficult to convince those who had traditionally expressed themselves through physical force that democratic politics was a more valid and attractive means of articulation. Not surprisingly, Loyalist violence escalated in the aftermath of the failure of the Brooke Talks and reached the point when, in 1992, Loyalists were responsible for more deaths than the IRA. It was clear that the situation was grave but we were finding it difficult to make headway in our efforts to promote political direction within the Loyalist community. Meanwhile, the British and Irish governments were trying to reconstruct the talks process. Sir Patrick Mayhew, the former British Attorney General, replaced Peter Brooke as Secretary of State for Northern Ireland and successfully reconvened inter-party negotiations among the same four parties as before. The Mayhew Talks began almost a year to the day after the Brooke Talks and lasted some six months. While the content of this round of talks was more comprehensive than the previous initiative, there was still little progress toward middle ground.

The Irish government and the SDLP were completely intransigent over some of the main issues, including Articles Two and Three of the Irish constitution. These claimed jurisdiction over the territory of Northern Ireland – territory legitimately held by another nation. Indeed, it had been ruled by the Irish courts that the territorial claim was a "constitutional imperative." This aggressive claim by the Republic of Ireland over a constituent part of the United Kingdom was of huge offense to the Unionist community and made relationships between Unionists and the Irish government hostile to say the least.

The Ulster Unionist Party broke political ground by agreeing to meet with the government of the Republic of Ireland in Dublin as part of the negotiations, but expectations that this move would produce a political response from the Irish were mistaken. In addition, the UUP had its own problems. There was a divergence of views among its membership over the nature of Northern Ireland institutions, some arguing for a strong Northern Ireland Assembly with significant powers and others, including its leader James Molyneaux, preferring a more modest administrative institution with no legislative control. Even at the point when negotiations had begun, there was uncertainty within the UUP about what political strategy was being employed by its leadership. Equally, the relationship between Molyneaux and Ian Paisley was a sham, with very little high level debate taking place between the leaders of the two parties. I believed that the Unionist position had been weakened in the talks process by this lack of cohesion within Unionism. We were excluded from the negotiations but were in contact with representatives of both the UUP and DUP, but it was despairing to experience the hostility that existed between the parties and that they did not comprehend the danger this disunity posed to the Unionist cause. It was becoming obvious to us that there was a shift of alignment within Nationalism and determined efforts were under way to establish a common approach. A lot of activity was taking place behind the scenes to create a pan-Nationalist consensus between the SDLP, Sinn Féin and the Irish government. This, in fact, was a principal reason why the talks failed. The details were only to emerge later but John Hume did not think the talks process could achieve a lasting settlement because Sinn Féin was not included in the process and because of the continuation of violence. He and the Irish Taoiseach Albert Reynolds were involved in separate, secret discussions with Sinn Féin with a view to creating political conditions that would lead to a more inclusive talks process and to an IRA ceasefire. Hume was not enthusiastic about the 1992 talks because he had his eye on the private process in which he was involved and was prepared to see the talks run into the sand in the hope that a more suitable process could emerge a little further down the line.

It was to emerge later that the British government had also been involved in a secret dialogue with the IRA for a number of years. And, when both sets of liaison became public, it caused severe concern within Unionism. It reeked of conspiracy and revealed that John Major had deliberately misled his own parliament and the people of Northern Ireland. Loyalists were particularly worried about the emergence of pan-Nationalism and the manner in which it was taking place. We regarded the coming together of the SDLP, the Irish government, Sinn Féin and by definition the IRA, which Gerry Adams had earlier described as the cutting edge of Nationalism, as the last push to force Unionism into political arrangements that would remove Northern Ireland from the United Kingdom and deny its people their rights to determine their future freely.

A part of the backbone of the Republican strategy was to force the British government to withdraw unilaterally its commitment to maintain the union, regardless of the views expressed by the people of Northern Ireland. Sinn Féin had consistently refused to recognize the principle of consent which set out that the union with Great Britain would continue for as long as the people of Northern Ireland desired that to be the case. Republicans were not interested in a democratic resolution of the conflict which required consensus between Unionists and Nationalists. Sinn Féin argued that it was the British government's responsibility to persuade Unionists to embrace a united Ireland and, if it failed to do so, it should set a firm timetable for a British withdrawal. In a set of political proposals published in 1989, Sinn Féin had even suggested that those who were not happy in a unified Ireland could be given grants to resettle in Great Britain. The alignment of the SDLP and the Irish government with Sinn Féin opened a direct route to the British government for exactly those aims of bypassing Unionism. Thus, it is not surprising that the sense of alienation within the Unionist population increased as a result.

Towards the Downing Street Declaration

In 1993, I was contacted by an individual who suggested that we meet to discuss what he described as "a sensitive matter." The person was from the Republic of Ireland and I understood that he represented the government of the Republic. Ray Smallwoods, David Adams and I met this person in a Belfast hotel and he informed us that the Irish government was interested in opening a channel of communication with Loyalists and, specifically, with the UDA. The political circumstances at the time led us to be very wary of this approach. Details of the dialogue between Gerry Adams and John Hume and the emerging pan-Nationalist process involving the Irish government were deeply unsettling for Unionism as a whole. We were suspicious of the motive behind the process and skeptical about the value of becoming involved in what was perceived to be a partisan exercise. It seemed that the groundwork had been developed within Nationalism and this was an attempt to give some balance to their efforts by drawing Loyalists into conforming to a pre-set Nationalist agenda.

We informed the UDA of the approach that had been made and, after a period of time, the offer for dialogue with the Irish government was rejected. The dominant view was that there was little to be gained from attaching credibility to a Nationalist devised project that had thus far excluded Unionism. Having already set the stage by devising a strategy that would accommodate Nationalism and the IRA, neither the UDA nor we believed that the Irish were seriously interested in a political initiative that would be acceptable to both traditions in Northern Ireland.

Yet, while we remained deeply suspicious of political developments and the intentions of the IRA, we were still committed to promoting an opportunity for progress, and debate within Loyalism continued. A working group had been established to examine the potential for creating a framework for political movement. The Loyalist Political Alliance was an informal body, which comprised three representatives each from the UDP and the PUP. The UDP delegation consisted of Ray Smallwoods, David Adams and myself. In addition, one representative from the UDA and one from the UVF took part. Both organizations were keen to be given an analysis of the developing political events and we were equally keen to appreciate the thought process within militant Loyalism in order to have a comprehensive understanding of the limits that existed for progress on a variety of fronts.

It was clear from the gradual exposure of the contents of the pan-Nationalist dialogue that the conditions for a settlement did not exist. It did not appear that the Irish, the SDLP and the IRA were prepared to accept that a settlement could not be imposed. Loyalists strongly wished for an environment that would create the conditions for progress toward an accommodative solution, but it did not seem that Nationalism was pulling in the direction of accommodation at all. Republicans continued to wage a fierce war against the Unionist community and against the state in an attempt to force Unionism and the British government to submit to constitutional change. The democratic rights of the Unionist population had no bearing on the militant Republican agenda.

The conflict continued to escalate during 1993; by autumn crescendo pitch had been reached, ushering in one of the most difficult periods of the entire Troubles. One act of violence in particular caused deep despair right across the community and precipitated another sharp upturn in intercommunal conflict. At lunchtime on October 23, the Shankill Road was shaken by an explosion. An IRA bomber had walked into Frizzell's Fish Shop carrying a holdall containing explosives. The bomb had an eleven-second timer designed to give the bombers enough time to escape before it exploded but, at the same time, to cause maximum death and injury to civilians.

The Shankill is the Loyalist heartland in Belfast and, on that day, it was swarming with people out doing their shopping. It was a Saturday, the busiest day of the week. The bomb exploded prematurely as its bearer, Thomas Begley, set it down.

He was blown to pieces, his accomplice was wounded and with them nine innocent people were murdered and fifty-seven injured. The entire building collapsed and people had to tear through the rubble with their bare hands in search for survivors, mostly in vain. The owner of the fish shop, Dessie Frizzell, was killed, along with his twenty-nine-year-old daughter, Sharon. Michael Morrison died with his partner Evelyn and their seven-year-old daughter, Michelle. Thirteen-year-old Leanne Murray was killed; George and Gillian Williamson and Wilma McKee also died. This terrible act of sectarianism shocked the world and it brought inevitable revenge attacks. In the space of one week, twenty-three lives had been claimed by the Troubles.

The Shankill bomb raised sharp questions about how, on one hand, Nationalists talked of opportunities for peace and, on the other, the IRA was killing women and children purely because of their religion. What caused even greater anger was the scene of Gerry Adams carrying the coffin of the Shankill bomber, Thomas Begley. He bore Begley's remains on his shoulder as a mark of respect for the person inside who had consciously set out to murder Protestants on the Shankill Road. A patriot in Gerry Adams' eyes, the coffin was draped with an Irish tri-color flag and an IRA black beret and gloves lay on top of it. It was a sickening sight to behold. These were dark hours for Northern Ireland and I found this period extremely depressing. It was becoming increasingly difficult to convince myself that any real progress was possible, but we continued to work on setting out the conditions for political advancement.

In late 1993, the Combined Loyalist Military Command set out six principles that it considered to be basic parameters that could provide a basis for an accommodative settlement. For agreement to be reached on the creation of democratic institutions which could command the support of both traditions, it was necessary to recognize basic rights. Loyalists envisaged a new political arrangement that would replace the Anglo-Irish Agreement with democratic structures that would allow both Nationalists and Unionists to cooperate within a framework founded on certain basic principles. The Six Principles, as they were known, described commitments that Loyalists were prepared to make in the interest of moving toward a political resolution of the conflict. They were as follows:

1. There must be no diminution of Northern Ireland's position as an integral part of the United Kingdom, whose paramount responsibility is the moral and physical well-being of all its citizens.
2. There must be no dilution of the democratic procedure through which the rights of self-determination of the people of Northern Ireland are guaranteed.
3. We defend the right of anyone or group to seek constitutional change by democratic, legitimate and peaceful means.
4. We recognize and respect the rights and aspirations of all who abide by the law, regardless of religious, cultural, national or political inclinations.
5. We are dedicated to a written constitution and Bill of Rights for Northern Ireland wherein would be enshrined stringent safeguards for individuals, associations and minorities.
6. Structures should be devised whereby elected representatives North and South could work together, without interference in each other's internal affairs, for the economic betterment and the fostering of good neighborly relations between both jurisdictions in Ireland.

This, in my view, represented a fundamental commitment on the part of Loyalism that it was prepared to contribute to the creation of an opportunity to move beyond the conflict if others would accept that challenge, despite a serious level of Unionist hostility to the political direction being taken by pan-Nationalism. It was also an attempt to demonstrate that common ground could be sought between the two traditions, regardless of our differences. Yet there was a deep lack of confidence in the whole ethos of the secretive process, which we were aware was underway. The public relationship between John Hume and Gerry Adams and the private one between Adams and the Taoiseach Albert Reynolds, not to mention the secret liaison between the British government and Sinn Féin, made it very difficult to contemplate an honorable and trustworthy peace initiative.

The major problem that dogged the peace process following the IRA and CLMC ceasefires right through the period up to the peace agreement in April 1998, and still today, was that the peace process, when it took public form, was unable to command sufficient cross-community confidence. The sense of common ownership of the process, which in a divided society is a prerequisite for its success, was not as complete as it should have been. The reason for this was that neither Reynolds nor Hume recognized that their objective to promote fundamental change in the approach of Republican extremists and lure them into the democratic process, was isolating Unionism because it was seen as a narrow Nationalist agenda. This was to prove a huge blind spot for the peace process as it developed. Sinn Féin was not concerned at all whether Unionism was alienated, because it did not accept that a peace settlement was based on the need for Unionist support. But Reynolds' and Hume's blind fixation with bringing Sinn Féin on board almost ruined the opportunities that were to be created farther down the line.

Parallel to the Hume–Adams dialogue, Albert Reynolds and John Major were contriving the text for what was to become the Downing Street Declaration. The link between the two initiatives, however, ensured that the Declaration was doomed from the beginning. A large section of Unionists refused to view it as anything other than a translation of the secretive process which had the IRA at its center regardless of the actual contents of the document. Reynolds too saw it as reflecting the discussions within Nationalism and Republicanism, confirming Unionist suspicions. The historical distrust of Anglo-Irish policy consequently was unlikely to diminish as a result of a document that was perceived to have the fingerprints of Gerry Adams and John Hume all over it. This was especially so since Northern Ireland is in essence a zero-sum society and what is good for Nationalists is perceived to be bad for Unionists, and vice versa. Secret liaisons with the IRA leading to a joint-governmental political initiative would hardly have the Unionist population jumping for joy. There was nothing to indicate that anything in which the IRA was involved would bring an honorable settlement any closer to Unionists.

While Unionists rejected the Downing Street Declaration, Loyalists were willing to explore any political development that had the potential to move the situation forward, but were not convinced that what was emerging could do that. Public opinion was not favorable, as the perception that the sole interest of both governments and the SDLP was to court Republicans and to appease the IRA grew. Yet Loyalists believed that no situation was unsalvageable until it clearly was and had produced the Six Principles as a challenge to all concerned and to set firm parameters to be heeded if a political initiative were to have any credibility. Developments thus far had done little to enthuse those within our community but we were used to the ham-fisted way in which the governments and others handled such things. Loyalists were merely trying to make a contribution to putting the boat on a more even keel before the governments capsized it completely.

I was aware that, while the channel offered by the Irish government some time earlier had been rejected by the UDA, some other vehicle for communication had emerged. It was more of a sounding board than anything else. The Reverend Roy Magee had, under the encouragement of the Primate of the Church of Ireland, Dr. Robin Eames, conveyed to the Irish government the danger of ignoring Unionist and Loyalist views. He had also been providing the UDA with an understanding of the views of the Irish government from time to time, but it was not a formal linkage. If that was what they wished, a solid relationship could easily have been established.

The Six Principles published by the CLMC were a matter of public record. There had been no effort to convey them secretly to either the British or Irish government as Loyalists wished their role to be transparent and free from misinterpretation. It would not be in our interests for it to be construed that

Loyalists were providing a veneer of balance to the pan-Nationalist agenda.

The government of the Republic was aware that there was strong Loyalist and Unionist concern about what Albert Reynolds was doing. Reynolds attempted to address that by incorporating some of the principles outlined by the CLMC into the text that became the Downing Street Declaration. When the Declaration was produced by Reynolds and Major on December 16, 1993, Loyalists studied it intensely. It was clearly a carefully worded instrument that sought to lay out the ground-rules for a future political settlement, but it was so carefully crafted that it seemed to be all things to all men. There were obvious overtones designed to win support within Republicanism as well as those reaffirming earlier commitments to Unionism. As a whole, however, the document was somewhat ambiguous. The CLMC concluded that it could not accept or reject the document, choosing instead to note its existence as a step toward opening space for greater debate. The UDP took a similar approach. The Declaration was not overly to our liking but it was not in our interest to kill it off immediately; rather we opted to wait and see what might evolve.

We also wanted to study the reaction of Republicans to the document, which indeed turned out to be a revelation. Over a lengthy period running into the spring of 1994, Sinn Féin was non-committal about the contents of the Downing Street Declaration and finally found it impossible to endorse as it obviously lacked some of the characteristics which Republicans had hoped it would include. In particular, the endorsement of the consent principle put the prospect for political and constitutional change firmly in the context of agreement by the majority of people in Northern Ireland, which meant that Unionist support had to be earned. Moreover, and not surprisingly, their demand that there should be a commitment from the British government to become persuaders for the reunification of Ireland as well as a timetable for a unilateral withdrawal from Northern Ireland, was not included. The expectation that these were matters of serious consideration raises questions about the level of sophistication within the Republican movement. Forced unification and a complete abandonment of the democratic wishes of the majority of people in Northern Ireland would have without doubt led to civil war. Loyalists had already provided ample evidence of their commitment to defend the rights of their community and of their capacity to resist the Republican war machine militarily.

Following the release of the Downing Street Declaration, I wrote to Albert Reynolds on behalf of my party asking for clarification on a number of points relating to his government's intentions toward Northern Ireland and its attitude toward the legitimate democratic rights of its people. The response, which I published along with the rest of the correspondence in the interest of transparency, was less than favorable. He was careful to be sensitive in his language but did little to earn confidence in my community. Simply put, the position of his government was to pursue the reunification of Ireland. In contrast, the British government argued that it had no selfish strategic or economic interest in Northern Ireland. Consequently, the problem remained that we found it difficult to accept that the Irish government could be considered a facilitator of a peace process alongside the British government when it was clear that both were coming from different basic positions. The British government maintained that it would not push the people of Northern Ireland in a particular direction but would allow them to choose their future freely. It considered itself neutral, while the Irish government was unashamedly partisan, its stated agenda being the reunification of Ireland.

Despite reservations about the Downing Street Declaration, the CLMC started to consider moves toward peace in December 1993. The possibility of calling an open-ended ceasefire over the Christmas period was raised with a view toward extending that cessation into the New Year if the conditions – in essence an IRA Christmas ceasefire – were correct. The CLMC believed that calling and extending a Loyalist ceasefire would apply pressure on the Provos to follow suit and extend their cessation as well. Effectively, the situation would have been manipulated so that Loyalists and Republicans could both independently end their hostilities and bind each other into a cessation of undetermined length. Under those circumstances, the first to return to violence would lose credibility worldwide. It was perhaps a little machiavellian and a long shot, but it was a gauntlet which would be thrown down to Republicans and to all concerned that, if violence was on hold from both sides, an opportunity for political movement could be created. There was no real point following the 1991 example of a one-sided halt to violence so the idea of taking advantage of the Christmas cease-fire period to manufacture a new situation seemed worth a try. We were enthusiastic about the idea but the IRA got wind of it and blew it out of the water. It released a statement saying that it would stop killing Loyalists if Loyalists stopped killing Nationalists but that the Republican campaign against the police and army would continue. This was a deliberate move to scupper any chance of an end to violence, for Loyalists could not possibly call an end to their hostilities in response to a mere scaling down of the IRA's campaign. As a result, the opportunity was destroyed.

This was yet another sign that Republicans were not serious about finding an honorable peace settlement. The CLMC soon thereafter stated that, while they were "preparing for peace," they were "ready for war." The next few months saw steady political activity and, as we drew closer to the summer of 1994, we continued to experience the dichotomy of a growing undercurrent of movement toward building the conditions for an end to hostilities while, on the surface, the war raged intensely. It was often difficult to square the circle in this respect and comprehend how the two could survive in tandem. The level of violence made it problematic to encourage people to think in the context of a post-conflict scenario, while they were witnessing the war being cranked up, not wound down. But there also was increasing community pressure to find a way to break the cycle precisely because of the horrific toll of the conflict at that point. The situation was getting out of control and, in both the Unionist and Nationalist sections of the community, there was abject despair for the future.

The building blocks for a change of IRA tactics were fitting into place. The signs suggested to us that the political focus was increasingly on a halt to IRA violence. Unionism was dominated by fears that serious political concessions were being afforded to Republicans in return for a cessation at some point. Meanwhile, there was little evidence that a balanced approach was being taken. Unionism was becoming increasingly alienated by a process that it perceived to be fixated solely on appeasing Republicans. Despite the unconducive environment, the UDP leadership continued to push for a pragmatic approach to the situation.

True, it did not seem that the British government was dealing with Unionism in good faith and the signals were that they were actually negotiating a ceasefire with Republicans. The fact that no such attention was given to Loyalist armed groups in itself exacerbated the belief that the dice were loaded. But, if all strands of Unionism were to stand together and share a common strategy, then, in our view, the Unionist position was unassailable. There was no prospect of Loyalist compliance with a process that was designed to overrule the democratic rights of the people of Northern Ireland. We did not trust the intentions of the IRA/Sinn Féin or those of the other players in the secretive process that had been going on. We did, however, trust our own integrity and ability to challenge any attempt to coerce us into an unacceptable arrangement, if Unionists would work together. That was the problem. The history of cohesion among the different parts of Unionism was less than impressive. The derisory attitudes of some Unionist figures toward my party and toward organizations such as the UDA, as well as the experiences of attempts at manipulation of paramilitaries by the Unionist leadership – relying on them at times of crisis and then denouncing them – all served to make relationships cool to say the least. It was not easy to get dialogue going between all the different parties and groups but we managed to do so in an unofficial way.

In 1994, meetings took place between representatives of the DUP, UUP, UDP, PUP and other Loyalist figures. The purpose was to explore whether there were areas of common concern where we could adopt a similar approach despite our differences. These meetings were not publicized as some of the senior political figures that attended had been adopting a public position of non-recognition of the UDP, and would have found it embarrassing to find attention drawn to the composition of some elements of the gatherings. We did not like this arrangement but accepted it in the greater interest of Unionism.

Ray Smallwoods' Murder

On July 11, 1994, I was driving to work when I got a very disturbing phone call. Since January, I had been working as an insurance salesman and traveled each morning to my office in Belfast city center. That morning, I had picked up my colleague from his house which was on my way, and I had also given a lift to one of his relations who needed a ride into the city. My colleague asked me what was wrong when I came off the mobile phone. "Ray has been shot," I told him. My aunt had called me because the news had traveled fast to my grandparents, who lived in an estate very close to where Ray lived. The details were sketchy. She thought he had been shot at the post office nearby when it had just opened at 9 a.m. She did not know how serious it was but would let me know as soon as she heard any details. I dropped my companions off in the city center and rushed straight back to Lisburn toward Ray's home. My phone was ringing constantly with people calling to tell me the news or to find out what I knew. By the time I got to Lisburn, I had no idea which of the competing rumors were true, but it became clear very quickly. The end of Ray's street was sealed off with white tape and the police and army were there. A crowd had gathered outside the cordon, anxious and curious about the incident. I climbed out of my car and was about to ask one of the policemen to let me through when I saw Jock, one of Ray's close friends. He told me very emotionally that Ray was dead. They had shot him outside his home, while his wife, Linda, watched on, and he had died on the way to the hospital.

I found it very difficult to absorb this information. In the course of my journey, after hearing the initial news, I had tried to prepare myself for the worst but it was incredibly shocking to hear the words. Ray and I had been very close and had come through a lot together over the past few years. We had worked with each other but, more importantly, our professional relationship within the party was founded on a strong friendship. Ray had been a friend of my father and he had holidayed with us when I was just a kid. I still have the photos of us all on the Isle of Man. My mother kept a close friendship with him when he was released from prison. It was then that I had gotten to know him, for he approached me as a friend of our family and reacquainted himself with me. He was still in prison when my father was murdered and when he came to see us after his release we struck up a firm and immediate friendship. He also became involved in the UDP, almost immediately proving to be one of the most dedicated and committed individuals I have ever had the pleasure to meet. I built up an immense respect for him over those few years before he was murdered.

What affected me most about his death was not just the tragic horror of losing a friend, or the sadness of the death of yet another colleague, but the utter cynicism of it. It caused me to question fundamentally whether there was any point trying to break out of this conflict. The role that Ray had been playing at that very crucial time was one that should have earned him reverence as he struggled to bring peace to our society in the most dangerous and challenging of environments. Instead, it earned him two cartridges from a sawn-off shotgun because the IRA saw his peace efforts as a threat to them. The similarity to my father's death was significant to me. I was convinced, then more than at any other time, that Republicans did not want an honorable peace with my people. Instead, they were striving purely for strategic advantage as they prepared to shift the emphasis of their struggle from armed to tactically unarmed conflict. This view was further reinforced when the IRA sought to murder me a few short days before the announcement of the Republican ceasefire in August. Luckily, I was warned of the attack and was able to evade their death squads.

Despite Ray's murder, the search for a solution to the conflict was not abandoned. Father Alex Reid and Father Gerry Reynolds from the Falls Road's Clonard Monastery decided to attend Ray's funeral and made public comments about Ray's efforts to bring peace, in order to keep the dialogue going. We had been engaged in a process of discussion with them and other church leaders for some time. Father Reid himself played a particularly interesting role at the time, as he had also been central to the process of discussion ongoing between Adams and Albert Reynolds over the course of the previous three years, shuttling back and forth from West Belfast to Dublin. I think his and Father Gerry Reynolds' presence at the funeral was a recognition that they deplored the motivation behind this murder.

There had never been a case of our discussions with Father Reid, or the wider church group of which he was a part, being a conduit for negotiation with Sinn Féin, although, had it been publicized at the time, some would have jumped to that conclusion. It was carefully constructed to ensure that this mechanism was not contrived as a channel for communication between Loyalists and Republicans. However, it was an extremely useful forum through which we could explore a better understanding of Nationalist and Republican thinking, which we were keen to do, and to promote greater awareness of Loyalism.

At the same time, we knew of Father Reid's role in the backdoor process within pan-Nationalism, though not from his own admission. Similarly, I know he and others were aware of the role Ray had been performing. And the Provos knew. That was why they killed Ray Smallwoods. The IRA cessation was imminent and we were aware of that and even had a reasonable understanding that it would be sometime in August. The escalation of IRA activity over the preceding months supported the anticipation that there would be a storm before the lull. Meanwhile, the Provos had taken a decision to eliminate the possibility of Loyalism stealing the march on them, just as they had done the previous Christmas, but this time by literal elimination.

In a period of a few weeks, the IRA placed bombs in Loyalist social clubs and murdered a number of Loyalists. They shot at the home of the Reverend William McCrea, a hard-line DUP Member of Parliament. They also shot dead two Protestant men on the Ormeau Road in Belfast, shooting one of them eighteen times. The IRA wanted to provoke an intense Loyalist response. The reason was to ensure that not only would they remove the risk of Loyalists beating them to it in the ceasefire stakes but they actually wanted Loyalist violence to roll on after their own cessation to give them maximum standing as peacemakers while Loyalists would be seen as peace-breakers and lose credibility. They also wanted to remove our political leadership and undermine our potency.

The massive backlash which the Provos sought did not materialize, mainly because Loyalists recognized what was going on and were not keen to play into the hands of Republican strategists. But I know there was a lot of anger out there and the thirst for revenge was palpable. This factor played a part in the debate that led to the subsequent Loyalist cessation, with anti-ceasefire elements arguing that there was unfinished business to contend with.

I found the few months between July and October to be one of the most difficult periods in my life. There were times when I considered throwing in the towel, only then to see that something momentous was within reach. It was very hard for me to convince my family, who were putting pressure on me to quit; indeed, it was difficult to convince myself at times. I had lost a friend and was lucky not to have lost my own life. It is hard to think that what you are working toward can represent peace when your enemies who are allegedly working toward the same goal are trying to wipe you out. I was losing faith in the prospect that any honorable peace settlement could be reached. But, then again, I also knew that to give up was to let my enemies win. I did not believe that the IRA was genuinely seeking to make peace with me or my community, believing rather that it was merely pursuing its own twisted interpretation of peace, which was to manipulate political conditions in such a way that would satisfy Republicans. The forthcoming ceasefire was only a temporary shift in policy to see if they could achieve those conditions. I did not believe that what Republicans considered to be the conditions for peace were acceptable to most people in my country. They had no real understanding of what the conditions for an accommodative settlement were.

But what we were trying to achieve was not guided by a requirement to make peace with the IRA. In many ways, it was to move the process into a position where we could achieve peace in spite of the obstruction which the IRA posed. If Republicans could recognize that change could not be forced and that it was up to the people of Northern Ireland to reach an understanding based on the democratic wishes of its diverse community, then we could make peace with them. If they were not prepared to work toward an honorable settlement, then we would resist their attempts to contort the peace process into something that would make real peace unattainable. I was strongly of the view that, while Republicans had played a very smart game so far, using their dual strategy of fierce armed aggression on the one hand and maximizing their political power on the other to fulfill their agenda, it would be a different game entirely if they found themselves solely in the democratic arena. If they had to conform to democratic constraints and essentially compete on the same basis as everyone else, then they would be squeezed. Republicans had the farthest to travel in political terms if an accommodative settlement was to be achieved, and the challenge of whether they could make that journey was not one for Unionism but for them.

For twenty-five years, Republicans had been trying to force the British government to withdraw unilaterally from Northern Ireland by waging an aggressive terrorist campaign against the state and the population which disagreed with them. They had failed to do so in military terms. In the course of their attempt, however, they had acquired a unique status, which allowed them to pursue their objectives in whatever manner they wished, provided they had the resources to do so, independently of any other influence. They did not have to conform to any system other than that of their internal process. By moving from armed conflict into the political arena they no longer had that freedom and would have to learn to conform to democratic parameters. It was logical that, if a negotiating process was properly constructed around the principle of consent, Unionism would be in a stronger political position than it had ever been. The whole context of the Republican struggle would be fundamentally altered in the sense that they could not deal directly with the British. Political or constitutional change would only be achievable by agreement across the community. Republicans for the first time would be forced to accept that, in order to realize their objectives, they had to convince the Unionist people whose opinion they had studiously ignored over the previous quarter of a century.

I knew that there was a real chance that we could move our country toward peace and redefine the landscape of the conflict if the commitment was there to do so. With that knowledge, I could not possibly give up after we had spent so much energy chasing that very goal. To do that would have made everything that my father and Ray had worked for and what so many others had given their lives for absolutely meaningless. Looking back now, I don't think it was ever in my nature to quit and I could not have lived with myself if I had just walked away then. I had started this because I had made a promise to myself that my father did not die in vain. So I had to see it through.

As we expected, the IRA ceasefire came on August 31, and the scenes that accompanied it were hard to swallow. Hundreds of Republicans streamed up and down the Falls Road in cars and black taxis waving tri-colors and shouting slogans of victory. The triumphalist nature of the occasion did not encourage euphoria on the nearby Shankill Road or in any other Protestant area. Republicans were portraying the ceasefire as the last stage of their struggle, cementing fears that a deal had been cut in secret with the British government and that we were not seeing all of the picture. There was an air of despondency that was not surprising in the face of the way the process had evolved up to that point. As attitudes were still being characterized in terms of victory and defeat, building trust in the integrity of the process was difficult, never mind overcoming the insecurity created through generations of division.

It all rang hollow to keen observers. It seemed like a case of playing it up to one's supporters and raising peoples' expectations about what the ceasefire was going to achieve. But it works both ways. For while it gets people on board in one instance over time, as the reality is exposed, it endorses the views of the doubters and weakens one's base. I have found it best to be bluntly honest to supporters about the difficulties and risks that invariably accompany strategic decisions, and never present to my constituency a situation as something it is not.

The national evening newspaper, the *Belfast Telegraph*, carried the headline "IT'S OVER," but we did not see it that way. An absence of violence is not peace. An IRA ceasefire was not more important than the motives behind it or the strategy it might be part of. The mood within the Unionist community as a whole did not reflect the relief that was undoubtedly there for it was masked by uncertainty and suspicion. Besides, all the focus was on the IRA ceasefire alone. That did not make a successful peace process. It had to be part of a larger equation. So eyes began to turn to the Loyalist groups.

The CLMC Ceasefire

As speculation grew about Loyalist intentions, intense debate was taking place within the Loyalist paramilitary groupings. Differently structured, each organization had to proceed in its own way to consult its members and secure their support for the decision to end its armed resistance. It has been argued that a ceasefire was inevitable because Loyalist hostilities were mainly reactive to Republican violence. That is not the case. It was extremely difficult to bring the CLMC to a point where all the component parts agreed that they would end hostilities. By no means was it an easy ride and I understand that, even when the decision to announce a cessation was reached, there were elements within all of the groups which remained unconvinced that it was the right step. Some of these people, mostly from within the UVF, later split away to form the Loyalist Volunteer Force, a disparate fanatical organization that set out to destroy the peace process, and subscribed to an ideology close to that of Ian Paisley's DUP.

I played almost no part in the internal consultation process within the UDA, except to offer analysis when requested, and that was infrequent. We had access to the highest level of that organization because of the unique liaison facility we had developed, but decisions of fundamental character under contemplation at that point were subject to the endorsement of the entire membership and that was mainly off limits to the UDP. It was their decision to make and I could not make it for them, nor would I have wanted to. In many ways, I could only look on powerlessly while the leadership deferred its own judgments to its rank and file. The UDA took longer than the UVF to reach a conclusion because of the extensive nature of its internal debate and its huge size, said to number more than 20,000 members.

The CLMC publically set out a number of issues that influenced its judgment on what strategic approach to take at that time, including questions related to whether deals had been made with the IRA to secure a cessation, the integrity of that ceasefire and the intentions of other armed Republican groups like the INLA which were not on ceasefire. I, along with a representative of the PUP, met an official of the British government in secret within days of the CLMC statement to discuss the elements that related specifically to the British position.

Making informed judgments on the areas of concern outlined previously by the CLMC left a lot to chance, and in many respects there was no other logical position to take than testing the commitment and intent of others to the process. There were no guarantees that the IRA would not return to war, or that deals had not been done behind everyone's backs, or whether there would be attempts at coercion on the part of the British or Irish government in the weeks and months ahead. If a sinister agenda existed, however, that would be exposed over time. The act of putting a toe in the water in 1994 was a delicate one, and one which was likely to be quickly withdrawn if threatening agendas were revealed.

There is no question of the ceasefire having been irreversible. If it shaped up that there was a serious threat to the Unionist community by either violent aggression or political coercion, I have no doubt that the ceasefire would have ended. This was something that not surprisingly emerged from the consultation process, and had to be revisited seventeen months later when the IRA revoked its ceasefire. On that occasion, Loyalists decided not to enter the fray immediately, despite having spelt out in the 1994 ceasefire declaration that their cessation was as permanent as that of the IRA, but that was because of changes in attitude that developed over the seventeen month period.

The last consultation in the overall process was with the political prisoners. A special meeting was arranged in the Maze prison to allow dialogue to take place with representatives of the prisoners. They had already consulted each prisoner on each wing of the H-Blocks. I was not invited to attend this meeting though I would later regularly visit the Maze prison to converse with the political prisoners. Their views were very important to the organizations and carried a lot of weight because these individuals had given up their freedom for the protection of the Loyalist people.

I received a phone call asking me to be at a certain location that evening. I arrived at the agreed time, along with some of my UDP colleagues, and was informed that the UDA had decided to end its campaign. The other components of the CLMC had been informed and they were going to meet in order to deal with the preparations for the announcement. While I was relieved by the result of the long-running debate and that our view had prevailed, I was uncomfortable with the speed in which they intended to proceed to an announcement. I have to confess that I argued against the public declaration of a ceasefire so quickly, which did in fact take place as planned three days later. I argued that more could be done to strengthen the Loyalist position and to prepare more adequately for some of the issues that had to be tackled. I was not satisfied that enough had been done to ensure that the process would move quickly to a recognition of the legitimacy of the UDP and to establish a forum for political negotiations on a way forward.

I foresaw problems and did not feel that the timing was quite right. It made no difference in terms of violent activity. No one's life would have been endangered by delaying the announcement by a week or two. Loyalist actions had effectively been on hold for six weeks already. But the leadership of the UDA was adamant that the ceasefire would be declared as quickly as was practicable. One of them told me that he understood my concern that more time was required but said, "Son, you will just have to work with the tools you are given." And that was that.

On the morning of Thursday October 13, a delegation comprising the UDP and the PUP held a press conference in Fernhill House at Glencairn, set in the hillside just above the Shankill. A huge old building sitting on elevated ground, it was surrounded by an expansive green area and looked down over the city. Its grounds had been used to train local men who had volunteered to fight for the British Army in the First World War. Now it is a museum that catalogs the role played by the people in the area during that terrible conflict. It was fitting that it was chosen as the place from which to announce the end of war that morning. We had been issued with a prepared statement by the Combined Loyalist Military Command and had been asked to present it to the press and the world. I spoke first, telling those gathered of the determination of the Loyalist community to build a fair and equitable society and build democratic structures that could provide a platform for lasting peace among our peoples. I pointed to the futility of the IRA's campaign of bloodshed over the past quarter of a century and how it had failed to beat the people of Northern Ireland into submission. But the assembled throng of media, more than I had ever found myself before, was interested only in the impending CLMC statement. The conference was broadcast live around the country. They waited with anticipation as I concluded my remarks and handed over to Gusty Spence who had been tasked with delivering the text of the cessation. The statement read as follows:

> *After a widespread consultative process initiated by representatives from the Ulster Democratic and Progressive Unionist parties, and after having received confirmation and guarantees in relation to Northern Ireland's constitutional position within the United Kingdom, as well as other assurances, and, in the belief that the democratically expressed wishes of the greater number of people in Northern Ireland will be respected and upheld, the CLMC will universally cease all operational hostilities as from 12 midnight on Thursday the 13th October 1994.*
>
> *The permanence of our ceasefire will be completely dependent upon the continued cessation of all Nationalist/Republican violence; the sole responsibility for a return to war lies with them.*
>
> *In the genuine hope that this peace will be permanent, we take the opportunity to pay homage to all our fighters, commandos and volunteers who have paid the supreme sacrifice. They did not die in vain. The Union is safe.*
>
> *In all sincerity, we offer the loved ones of all innocent victims over the past twenty-five years, abject and true remorse. No words of ours will compensate for the intolerable suffering they have undergone during this conflict.*

Let us firmly resolve to respect our differing views of freedom, culture and aspiration and never again permit our political circumstances to degenerate into bloody warfare.

The part that attracted most attention was the expression of remorse, which I regarded as a genuine gesture to underscore the heartfelt desire on the part of the CLMC to put the war behind us all. The IRA had singularly failed to show any sign of compassion or regret when it had halted its campaign six weeks before. That was a distinction that was remarked upon and was a characteristic of the years ahead and the difficulty in overcoming issues of distrust, hurt and sincerity. I thought that it was an important element in the confidence-building process that the CLMC had tried to reach out to the Nationalist community by acknowledging the hurt it had caused as a result of the conflict.

On the Road to Peace

Five days after the ceasefire, I was in the United States of America along with five other colleagues from both the UDP and PUP. We had been invited by Bill Flynn, President of the Mutual of America insurance company and Chairman of the National Committee for American Foreign Policy, based in New York. He had been involved, along with others such as Niall O'Dowd, in encouraging the Clinton administration to take an active interest in the political developments in Northern Ireland. We traveled to New York, Boston and Washington telling our story about Loyalism and attempting to promote an understanding of the Unionist position. It caused criticism in our own constituency because Unionism's generic view of America and particularly Irish Americans was one of meddlesome people who are exclusively Nationalist and naïve with respect to the realities of Northern Ireland. In many ways that view is understandable as the IRA for years peddled lies and propaganda within the Irish-American community to gain financial support to buy guns for its campaign. But what we had here was an invitation to explain another side of the story. Our side. Unionists had not gone to America to address the misunderstandings or to tackle the Republican propaganda machine. Whether we liked it or not, the US administration had become a serious player in the context of the peace process and we had to ensure that it was informed of the Unionist position.

Those who encouraged us to come to the United States were undoubtedly Nationalist in their outlook and unashamedly so. They were also genuinely interested in hearing what we had to say and I am glad they were and still are. People such as Niall, Bill, Tom Moran and Ed Kenny became friends who were willing to expose American audiences to a point of view that was radically different and challenged their views. Some months later, at the White House St. Patrick's Day reception in 1995, Niall O'Dowd asked me to write a column for his New York publication, *The Irish Voice*, in order to introduce his readership, which would be exclusively Nationalist, to an opposing Loyalist voice. He did not have to do that and I think he took a risk that other publishers in smaller markets might not have taken. It must have worked all right because he later asked me to write a weekly column for *Ireland on Sunday* when he launched that newspaper at the end of 1997.

Following the ceasefire, I gave up my job and began work with the party on a full-time basis. The workload and responsibility that we had taken on could no longer be shouldered by part-time activists. There was a lot to be done as the UDP was catapulted from relative obscurity into the very center of the political arena. We were responsible for contributing an analysis of the views and attitudes, not just of our electorate but also of the position of the UDA. The PUP had a working relationship with the UVF and therefore it performed a similar role. Between us, we became the political personification of Loyalism. Our objective was to move the peace process to a point where all-party negotiations could take place on new democratic structures that would reflect the diversity of our society and put power and responsibility for Northern Ireland's affairs back into the hands of its people. In order for such a negotiation process to have the optimum chance of reaching a successful conclusion, it was important that all relevant interests felt able to contribute to the process. In that respect, we held a relevance to the process that stretched beyond our electoral mandate as we were the only people who could give political expression to those who had previously expressed themselves through physical force. It was in our interest and everyone else's to ensure that the paramilitary groups were committed to making the process work and were locked into democracy. Sinn Féin has the same relevance because of its relationship with the IRA – whether or not the party acknowledges it.

The pursuit of negotiations was complicated by the fact that the British government and some of the Unionist parties refused to recognize my party or the PUP. We were denied the facilities open to other political parties, such as access to government representatives or ministers. We were treated as if we were nonpersons. I was the leader of a political party which had an electoral mandate and elected representatives and had consistently played a constructive role in the fight to bring an end to violence in our country. We had never supported violence and our opposition to violence had gone beyond the party rhetoric we heard from others. We actively and successfully promoted a change in approach, which resulted in an end to conflict. Still we were not treated like a legitimate political force. We had to go through a process termed "exploratory dialogue" which was a test phase of decontamination in which we would have discussions with civil service representatives and the government would decide if it was appropriate for us to be treated as democrats. This was insulting and humiliating, but we jumped through these hoops nonetheless, using these meetings to impress upon the government a strong Loyalist agenda that we believed would assist the resolution of the conflict.

In March of 1995 we were given access to ministers of government but it was not until after the 1996 forum elections from which the negotiations were convened that we were afforded the same rights as other political parties. Nevertheless, some continue to discriminate against us. To this day, Ian Paisley's DUP refuses to hold official meetings with us, which is curious considering the fact that we have met some of its most senior figures in other circumstances, privately, at the height of Loyalist violence.

We expected that a negotiation process would emerge at an early stage following the ceasefires, but that was not to be the case. The main Unionist parties did not view the circumstances within the context of conflict resolution. Instead, they favored a different approach, which was to pursue political progress involving only the political parties that had traditionally been involved in the Brooke/Mayhew Talks. That was a failure to recognize the reality of what was required to find a way sensibly to overcome our political divisions and, from a Loyalist perspective, was a juvenile position. In the absence of a formal negotiation body into which all relevant factions were locked and forced to conform, Unionism was in a weak position. Not only were Unionists affording Republicans a special status that allowed them to work directly with the British government which was exactly what Republicans wanted, they were also guaranteeing them international sympathy for what was seen as the disenfranchisement of Sinn Féin and its supporters, earning them political support and millions of dollars in financial aid. While we were not convinced that Republicans were genuinely seeking an accommodative settlement, the Unionist parties would not see that the only way to test that theory was to challenge them at the talks table. We were not afraid to challenge Sinn Féin and were the first to debate that party in public. As far as we were concerned, the bona fides of Sinn Féin/IRA could only be established by submerging them into the democratic process. But that is not how it transpired. Northern Ireland went through the wringer for almost two years before talks finally began and, in the course of that time, the IRA ceasefire collapsed and the peace process was brought to the edge more than once. We disagreed with the approach of the DUP and UUP in that period but we also recognized that people could not be forced to the negotiating table. It was a voluntary act that required confidence, and talks could never succeed unless those present around the table were willing to make them work. The atmosphere for negotiations was not right for different reasons but, thankfully, after many twists and turns, the peace process reached a positive outcome in April 1998 after two years of stumbling negotiations. Some of those twists and turns are described from my personal reflections at the time in the series of newspaper articles that follow. I hope they provide a flavor of the remarkable journey which the people of Northern Ireland have taken, balancing on a knife-edge in search of the peace they so richly deserve.

Part Two–1995

The year of 1995 was characterized by painfully slow progress and still all-party negotiations appeared no closer. In January, British troops ended daytime patrols and the British government lifted the ban on ministerial contact with Sinn Féin, the Ulster Democratic Party and the Progressive Unionist Party. In February, the Framework Document was released. In March, the UDP was the first Unionist party to attend the White House St. Patrick's Day reception. In May, a Northern Ireland investment conference in Washington attracted 1,300 delegates from all political backgrounds. In June, the British government renewed its anti-terrorism laws despite the Republican and Loyalist ceasefires, and the decommissioning of arms was made a pre-condition for negotiations. In July, the release of Private Lee Clegg and the re-routing of Orange marches sparked wide-spread violence. In August, James Molyneaux resigned as leader of the Ulster Unionist Party. In September, David Trimble was elected to succeed Molyneaux, and the UDP and Sinn Féin shared a platform for the first time. In November, US President Bill Clinton visited Northern Ireland for the first time and the British–Irish twin track initiative was launched. In December, the International Body headed by Senator George Mitchell, General John de Chastelain and former Norwegian Prime Minister Hari Holkeri set out to examine the arms issue. But, despite all efforts, the year ended without negotiations having begun.

■ ■ ■

We're a Long Way Off from Lasting Peace
(*Irish Voice* March 29–April 4, 1995)

On February 22, the document *A New Framework for Agreement* was released. It contained proposals for a one hundred and eight-seat Northern Ireland Assembly as well as the guiding principles for achieving cooperation between Nationalists and Unionists. One of these principles was that agreement could only be pursued by and established by exclusively democratic, peaceful means, without resort to violence or coercion. All Unionist parties, however, rejected the document as it had an all-Ireland ethos and did not adequately address the totality of relationships.

On October 13 of last year, the Ulster Democratic Party (UDP) and the Progressive Unionist Party (PUP) announced the cessation of Loyalist violence on behalf of the Combined Loyalist Military Command (CLMC). This event brought to reality the hope of an end to violent conflict in Northern Ireland.

Both my party and the PUP have become the political representatives of the Loyalist paramilitary groupings. The conflict in my country has been transformed from physical to political and we are playing our role in pursuing a fair and equitable political settlement for the people of Northern Ireland. I believe there is a firm realization that the best way forward for Northern Ireland and its people does not lie in armed conflict. There are, however, many obstacles to achieving a real and lasting peace.

Many think that we are already experiencing peace in Northern Ireland. I say we are merely no longer at war. The divisions between the two parts of the community, which have been accentuated through twenty-five years of conflict, firmly remain. Peace can only be achieved by encouraging dialogue. Unfortunately, life is complicated in my part of the world, and the fears and distrust that have dominated our experience make that very dialogue difficult. This is clouded even further by our exclusion from full participation in the political process by the government because of the retention of weapons by various groupings.

When I was in Washington DC recently, I met a number of politicians and representatives of the Clinton administration. There was, not surprisingly, one common thread to all these discussions – arms. The issue of disarmament is understandably high on the agenda, both in the States and at home. The message coming from the British, Irish and, indeed, the American governments is that weapons must be decommissioned. I sympathize with this desire. I want to see the guns taken out of politics, but this is an incredibly complex and difficult issue. It has become central to the "peace process," and progress is now conditional upon resolving the arms issue.

The belief that the paramilitary groupings must disarm before the process can move forward is nonsense. The issue cannot be dealt with in a vacuum. It is a simplistic attitude, and serves only to complicate the matter even further. It is my opinion that the decommissioning of weapons and war materials can only be achieved through building trust – trust between the paramilitaries, trust in the British and the Irish governments, and, most importantly, trust in the process itself.

I can speak only from a Loyalist perspective and Loyalism is deeply suspicious of the IRA and its objectives. The IRA has offered no mirror of the CLMC expression of "abject and true remorse" in their ceasefire announcement for the suffering inflicted upon the community. The IRA has yet to acknowledge that its actions over the past quarter of a century were even wrong. Their ceasefire decision is seen as a strategic rather than a moral one. Their intentions are unclear.

Indeed, while calling for all-party talks, the IRA continues to target people in the Protestant community and members of the police for potential assassination. They continue to train and equip themselves. This does not build trust. The IRA is seen to be holding a knife to the throat of the peace process. They are talking of peace, but are preparing for war.

Loyalists also fear the possible resumption of violence from other Republican groups. If things do not go their way, will splinter groups emerge? Evidence of this possibility lies in the placing of semtex bombs in border towns. There have been three such instances, the most recent on March 16 in Newry, Co. Down. Sinn Féin President Gerry Adams blamed the British government. The reality is that the IRA are the only group to have semtex explosives. This could be the work of a dissident faction within IRA ranks or a ploy to pressurize the British government into concessions. Whatever the case, Gerry Adams should be seen to come clean about the IRA's control over personnel and munitions.

This, of course, paints a very bleak picture, but these are very real and legitimate concerns for Loyalists. I think that it is important for everyone to be able to put their cards on the table. Republicans must understand my fears as I must understand theirs. This is part of the healing process. The difficulties that face us are not insurmountable, but they are challenging.

I think it is unfair to expect either side to relinquish its weapons until its fears and uncertainties can be allayed. Surely we can be thankful enough that the guns have remained silent for the past seven months. In the long run, I am convinced that the decommissioning of weapons will come about. Progress is necessary on other equally important issues to facilitate this. If one thing is certain, it is that peace cannot become a single-issue process.

The most pressing and important task ahead is not removing the guns, it is encouraging dialogue in order to find a political settlement that can command the support and trust of both sections of the community. Then there can be no excuse or reason for arms retention. Dialogue, however, must be inclusive. Those who have contributed to the conflict must be allowed to contribute fully to the search for a settlement. To exclude them from the process is insane. Yet the UDP, PUP and Sinn Féin are denied their equal place in the political arena. The confidence in the political process, which is itself the catalyst toward peace, is stymied because we are not truly part of it. The Framework Document produced by the British and Irish governments does not represent a full analysis or offer a basis for a solution, because our parties have been unable to contribute to it.

The British government should engage in dialogue with all the political parties and seriously consider all the proposals on the table. This will provide the necessary dynamic for progress and attain the commitment from all sides to see it through to its conclusion. Then, and only then, can we adequately start on a truly wholesome process whereby we can work toward overcoming fears and uncertainties that keep us from achieving a lasting peace.

Clinton's Conference Was Great; Adams/Mayhew Was a Sideshow

(*Irish Voice* May 31–June 6, 1995)

On May 24, a widely attended investment conference on Northern Ireland opened in Washington, DC. Vice President Al Gore, addressing the delegates at the gala dinner, called for an end to all political violence and punishment beatings. Media attention, however, focused on a private meeting between Sinn Féin President Gerry Adams and Secretary of State for Northern Ireland, Sir Patrick Mayhew.

I must say that I thoroughly enjoyed the White House economic conference in Washington last week. It served as an important demonstration of the US government's commitment to the peace process, which was consolidated by the intensity of participation in the conference and by the presence of the very top level of the US administration. President Clinton's oration to the conference was recognized by all as impressive and sincere.

The success of the conference cannot be accurately judged until we see practical evidence of investment, but there certainly appeared to be a feel good factor surrounding the event and I am optimistic that there will be real benefits for the economies of Northern Ireland and the border counties. The peace process in Northern Ireland depends not only upon finding a political way forward; equally important is the need to rebuild the economic base which has been destroyed by a quarter century of conflict. Disadvantage and unemployment must be tackled by developing industry and creating jobs.

The conference was indeed as it was described by many of the contributors – historic. Not just because of the opportunity it offered Northern Ireland for economic regeneration, or for the impressive support it attracted from the administration and American business world, but because it brought together all shades of political opinion from both Northern Ireland and the Republic of Ireland.

It was a curious experience to find everyone under the same roof. It demonstrated that common aims could transcend political differences. Even the Democratic Unionist Party (DUP) was there, albeit without its leader Dr. Ian Paisley, who boycotted the conference along with Jim Molyneaux, leader of the Ulster Unionist Party (UUP), because Sir Patrick Mayhew was to meet informally with Gerry Adams. Both Paisley and Molyneaux, however, managed to send the rest of their party hierarchies. Perhaps those they sent were less principled or they thought they could have their cake and eat it. Sometimes, it is hard to fathom such hypocrisy but, thankfully, this demonstration of Jurassic politics detracted only from their own credibility and not the conference itself. In fact, Paisley's and Molyneaux's absence went unnoticed by virtually everyone.

In comparison, the meeting between Adams and Mayhew was an unwelcome sideshow, which created a predictable media circus. I think it unnecessarily brought politics into the conference. Indeed, it was for this reason that I declined the invitation to engage the Northern Ireland Secretary in a similar way the next day.

After the Adams meeting there was an almost audible sigh of relief, and people wanted to get back down to business. There was no way we were going to set the merry-go-round in motion again. The meeting with Adams was pure PR and could have taken place back home. I firmly believe that there is a time for politics and a time for business. I was there to sell Northern Ireland, not to engage in glossy publicity stunts with no practical purpose.

The political message, which was latent and so much more effective than the cosmetic handshakes, was that the sands are shifting and that things are happening, quite naturally, with the evolving peace. It was strange enough to know that everybody was there at the conference, but it was positively bizarre to be able to watch the different shades of politics effortlessly work the room without any sign of discomfort.

I watched as Ulster Unionist MPs sat at one end of the bar, while Adams was a few feet away, each engaging in their own particular activities. This is something we would not have seen six months ago. Even though the DUP delegation was fleeting from room to room in strict formation and scanning the area with hands firmly in pockets lest they be compromised by some opportunist Republican, they were there and that is important.

Attitudes have changed indeed. When President Clinton invited representatives from all the Northern Ireland parties to the White House last St. Patrick's Day, I was the only Loyalist to attend. I believe that while there was criticism from predictable sources of the step which my party – the UDP – had taken, there wasn't the outcry from the community that might have been expected.

Perhaps this demonstration that people on the ground are prepared for some change gave encouragement to the UUP to take the initiative last month by sending Dr. Chris McGimpsey to debate with Sinn Féin's Gerry O'Hara in New York. This was an unexpected move, taken to break the platform ban on debates with Sinn Féin. Now we may see a similar step in Northern Ireland as an acknowledgement that people must be able to hear the views of both sides together, and for Unionism and Republicanism to debate their positions.

The investment conference was the next step, when all parties were in attendance both at the conference and at the White House reception. This was in sharp contrast to the position only two months earlier on St. Patrick's Day. I now have even read rumors in the newspapers that the UUP had informal discussions with Sinn Féin on social matters while at the conference. This may be erroneous but, in the surprising event of it being true, it would describe a distinct policy shift.

Changes are most certainly taking place. At a time when some of us are complaining about lack of pace in the process between ourselves and the British government, I look around and see some amazing movement on the horizon. Perhaps it points to an important issue. While parties such as ours have played a part by ending the violence, and continue to sustain the peace process, we should also encourage the other parties in their efforts to acclimatize themselves to the new atmosphere. We should acknowledge evidence of their success. Everyone has an equal responsibility to overcome difficulties ahead, and to take necessary risks to ensure that their voices are heard and that peace lasts.

Clegg Release Has Loyalists Angry Too
(*Irish Voice* July 5–11, 1995)

On July 3, Private Lee Clegg, who shot dead teenager Karen Reilly during a joyriding incident in 1990, was released after four years in custody. As a result, widespread rioting erupted in Republican areas. When the protest showed no sign of abating, the CLMC warned that "Republicans are playing a game of the highest stakes and appear prepared to test the peace process to its very limits."

The controversial decision to release Private Lee Clegg has thrown the proverbial cat among the pigeons. Neither Loyalist nor Republican groups are happy that this decision has been made in isolation. Private Lee Clegg is a political prisoner. He would not have committed the crime for which he was convicted but for the political situation. Indeed, he would not have been on the streets of Ulster at all.

It is with disappointment that we hear of Clegg's release. The government may be able to use this political decision as an appeasement to bolster support from the right wing Tory backbench at a time when John Major needs it most, but it has had a profoundly negative effect upon the peace process. All political prisoners should be given the attention Clegg has received. As part of the normalization process, all prisoners must be reviewed.

The Clegg release has provoked heavy disturbance in Nationalist West Belfast and in Londonderry. On Monday there was sporadic rioting and, most worryingly, a number of hijacked cars were abandoned in Loyalist areas, which prompted bomb scares. This has not been seen for almost a year, and is somewhat disconcerting. While initially the story of the day was the Clegg issue, now upon its back is a major concern that these disturbances signal a threat to the peace process.

The cynics may say that if a dog barks in the street in Belfast it is accused of threatening the peace process. But the harsh reality is that, if the situation gets out of control, there could be a knock-on effect on the ceasefire. Rioting is bad enough; bomb scares are very disturbing. How easy for the hoaxes to develop into real bombs, how easy for the riots to become punctuated by gunfire.

It is a very dangerous game to play right now at an already difficult juncture in the process. I would urge Sinn Féin to promote calm within their community. To engage purposely in such street politics at every bad turn does not augur well for the future of the process. What happens when the difficult decisions about our political future have to be made? And there will be many. Each time something does not go our way, will the heat be turned up and the peace process brought to the very edge? The language of confrontation must be replaced by that of compromise. But where is compromise?

I was listening recently to a radio program on Radio Ulster which had Martin McGuinness from Sinn Féin on live outlining his party's position. During the course of the program, someone from County Tyrone called and asked under what circumstances Sinn Féin would be prepared to accept a place in a local assembly. The reply was that Sinn Féin would only accept such a structure if there was a declaration of British intent to withdraw accompanying it.

I must say I was somewhat dismayed. Sinn Féin must move beyond the rhetoric and begin pursuing the politically achievable. McGuinness fails to acknowledge the principle of consent, maintaining instead a united Ireland or nothing position. This seems in sharp contrast to the statement from Sinn Féin *Árd Comhairle* (National Executive) member Jim Gibney who in May said that Republicans should be prepared to explore "compromise positions" with Unionists. He also said that "those of a Nationalist outlook must look for a new language in order to engage with the Protestant people of this land; it must be the language of invitation."

I have detected little usage of that language by Martin McGuinness. This is a historic opportunity to find peace; perhaps the last opportunity. Peace can only be achieved by compromise in this divided society. Flat insistence on a British withdrawal is not helpful. Considering that a sizable majority of the people of Northern Ireland consider themselves British, the suggestion that peace is conditional upon the destruction of the British state is insensitive if not offensive. Moreover, such cast-iron positions will keep us from settlement. Only when Nationalists learn to accept and respect the other community's culture, heritage and identity, and the Ulster British community do likewise, will we truly move forward. Any settlement must be based upon the recognition of both the Britishness and Irishness of those in our society, and must be able to accommodate both identities.

I am often confronted by skeptics who contend that it is impossible to visualize an agreement between Protestants and Catholics here. How can you reconcile the irreconcilable? I believe that accommodation is possible because I refuse to accept that the only possible solution is domination of one section of the community by the other through conflict. The peace process must be a process of conflict resolution, to help develop conditions for accommodation and reconciliation.

One problem which must be faced is that the peace process is developing along the wrong axis. The physical conflict between Republicans and the British government is replaced by one of political pre-conditions. The tactics have changed but the goal remains the same. The war will not be over until they get the "Brits out." Indeed, it seems to me that a great number of people are entirely missing the point about resolving this conflict. The conflict may be seen by Republicans as historically between the Irish and the British, but British rule has been a historical motivation for conflict which then became the rationale for its maintenance.

Getting the Brits out won't deliver peace. There are upwards of two thirds of the people in Northern Ireland who consider themselves British. They weren't airdropped into the province in 1969 – they have been here for a very long time and intend to remain. Peace can only be arrived at through dialogue and negotiation between Ulster Protestants and Ulster Catholics, those who have been in the cockpit of the conflict.

Yet, Sinn Féin continues to dwell in the past and refuses to recognize the legitimacy of my tradition. They have urged the British government to act as persuaders – to convince Unionists that their best future lies in a united Ireland. While Sinn Féin continues to focus on the government, it is merely deferring the real challenge which faces it. How is it going to fit the million or so Prods into its analysis?

If we are to search meaningfully for peace, then the core issue must be dealt with. That is, the relationship between the two traditions in Northern Ireland. Unless this relationship is addressed, any proposed settlement will fail. The government's declaration that it has no selfish strategic or economic interest in Northern Ireland was seen by many Unionists as a sign of abandonment. I, however, see it as a strong message to Nationalists that it is not the government with which they must resolve the conflict, it is with their cohabitants in this country, the Unionists.

We must find a formula which enables us to share this land, representing our joint heritage. To do so, we must recognize what is required of each of us. That is, to deal with the political realities of finding a settlement, and to address the obstacles to reconciliation posed by opposing analyses. In short, Loyalists need to hear more of Jim Gibney's new language and a lot less of Martin McGuinness' old rhetoric.

Moral Courage Needed to Save the Peace

(*Irish Voice* July 19–25, 1995)

Republican violence in response to the Clegg release was matched by Loyalist violence partially as a reaction to the perceived Republican threat but also in response to the stand-off between the RUC and the Orange Order at Drumcree. Northern Ireland descended into a spate of sectarian violence characterized by attacks on both Catholic and Protestant homes, as well as Orange Halls and Catholic schools.

The peace process appears to be deteriorating rapidly. Senior Republicans have described the process as being "in crisis" and I would not disagree. Over the past fortnight in particular, we have witnessed a series of difficulties and seen tensions rise to the surface: the release of Lee Clegg and the subsequent violence; the culmination of the re-routing issue; sectarian arson attacks on Orange Halls and businesses; confrontations with the police. Every day brings more problems. The question which must now be asked is: How much strain will the process take and what can be done to save it?

Ken Maginnis, the Ulster Unionist security spokesman, has accused the IRA of deliberately provoking confrontations and engaging in a rolling resumption of violence. It would be easy from a Loyalist perspective to buy into Maginnis' theory, in light of the clearly orchestrated spate of hijackings and rioting which has been sustained over the past two weeks.

Even before the Lee Clegg release, there were confrontations with the police in North Belfast every night for a week. To me, it seemed that the Clegg affair served as a pressure valve to vent the frustration which had been tangibly building up. And, on that basis, I was prepared to accept the overflow of violence. But this has been accompanied by bomb hoaxes in Loyalist towns, creating anxiety, and then guns appeared during the hijackings. Now every night there have been arson attacks on Orange Halls, business premises and Protestant homes. These are not actions which can be mistaken as frustration with the government but efforts aimed against the Protestant community. It is almost as if there is a policy of brinkmanship – seeing how far the peace process can be pushed until it breaks. The process has had a shaky lifespan for the past eleven months, but it is now passing through its most critical juncture. We are riding a roller coaster which can only end in conflict unless steps are taken to defuse the situation. On both sides of the divide there are frustrations surrounding the lack of movement toward resolving the cause of the conflict. A distinct absence of imagination has been displayed by the government toward post-conflict negotiations or the necessary normalization of society by the release of prisoners.

Sinn Féin complains that it has *little* to show for its efforts in bringing a cessation of violence: Loyalists have absolutely *nothing* to show. Rapid government movement on the prisoners issue would help to dissipate the anxiety in both camps. All paramilitary organizations must be provided with a practical and clear demonstration of the benefits of a continuing peace. This could give the peace process a temporary lifeline, but there must also be the prospect of inclusive negotiations.

The problems facing Northern Ireland can only be resolved through dialogue, but, somewhat perversely, the declining confidence in the peace process is making the possibility of dialogue even more difficult. Even if the government was to accede now to talks, it is unlikely that the main Unionist parties would agree to participate, given the present climate.

The intentions of Republicans and their commitment to peace are under question. The use of street violence at times of unease serves to punctuate fear that increased violence and the threat of an inevitable return to arms would be used as a lever at each turn if Republican objectives were not met. The direction of such violence toward the Loyalist community, as we have already seen, may have already eroded what little confidence had been built up in the IRA's willingness to compromise. Republicans must demonstrate their commitment to resolving the conflict, and acknowledge the need to overcome the fears which keep people from the negotiating table. In the interest of both communities, we must each understand the difficulties the other must circumvent and, perhaps, even help each other to do so.

Republicans are not making the job at hand any easier by allowing for a sustained assault upon the Protestant community. The sectarianism which is beginning to surface will be replicated by reprisal. As we should well know from recent history, violence begets violence. To allow such a spiral to evolve will surely sound the deathknell for peace in our country forever. History should be learnt from, not repeated. Moral courage is needed from those on both sides who facilitated the peace process, to ensure that it may last.

A Year of Peace, but Precious Little Progress

(*Irish Voice* September 6–12, 1995)

On August 31, 1995, Sinn Féin celebrated the first anniversary of the IRA cease-fire. Sinn Féin President Gerry Adams pledged that his party would look constructively at the issue of the decommissioning of arms and again called for all-party talks to begin immediately.

There is a firm tradition of marking anniversaries in Ireland. Every year, each side has religiously hit the streets and celebrated the memory of 1916 or 1690, and now both traditions add 1994 to the marching calendar. But when we reflect upon the ceasefires of August 31 and October 13, 1994, how much cause for celebration is there?

While we must indeed be thankful for the removal of the physical conflict, there has been precious little progress and the core issues of the conflict have not yet been addressed. We are no closer to settlement than we were one year ago and the euphoria of the ceasefires has been replaced by a profound uncertainty about what lies ahead. Indeed, it could be said that there was more hope and expectancy last year than exists now.

I don't think that it can be said that any one side has played the game particularly well. I think this is in part because we have not yet reached a stage where there is a common understanding of what the parameters and direction of the peace process should be. Each participant, while perhaps entering the process for the right reasons, has been selfish in the handling of it. Of course, we must seek to achieve our own goals within the peace process, but we must also, for the sake of the integrity of the process itself, understand obstacles which present themselves not only to us, but to others, and seek to overcome them.

The most central issue in the peace process is, of course, dialogue, for it is only through talks and negotiations that we can find a path toward an eventual resolution of the conflict and the establishment of a stable political arrangement. However, after one year of ceasefire, this dialogue is not taking place. Sinn Féin has placed the blame for this primarily on the British government, but that is somewhat unfair. Republicans, too, have done little to move us toward talks. I cannot ignore that throughout the past year they have consistently failed to show any understanding of the Loyalist position. I have repeatedly questioned the intentions of Republicans in this peace process. I wonder whether they wish to see a resolution to the conflict on anything but their own terms. They appear to seek movement only by force and by making the British government back down in the face of Republican pressure.

I do not believe that Republicans really accept that agreement must be found between the two traditions in Ulster, or that they should seek such agreement. Their attitude suggests that Unionists must be faced down, that the government must force Unionists to the table and that the inevitability of a British withdrawal and a future united Ireland must be accepted.

Unionists, however, will not go to the table if talks are called tomorrow. I think they are wrong to take this attitude, but this is the reality of the situation. The question is how do we address this problem? Sinn Féin's answer is to launch a campaign of disruptive street demonstrations. It is difficult to see how such action could encourage the Unionist parties to start negotiations. In fact, the result of such tactics is to make the possibility of such talks less likely. I believe that if the Unionist parties can be convinced that the time is right for such talks, then they will happen. But it is not the government who can convince them. I have such a responsibility, and I will endeavor to do so, but Sinn Féin also has this responsibility. Sinn Féin's policy of street politics begs the question, can they maturely engage in dialogue in a political process, or will they spill onto the streets every time they are unhappy? So far, Republican action has only been dangerous and unhelpful.

I also feel extremely frustrated by the attitudes of the Unionist parties toward the peace process as a whole. I find it difficult to fathom the thinking of those who have been quite comfortably hiding behind the violence of the past twenty-five years, using it as a shield from having to deal with the reasons why the conflict erupted in the first place. That shield has been removed, yet they seek to erect further barriers, again cushioning them from that challenge.

Unionist parties insist upon the decommissioning of arms before they will take part in talks. I can understand that this is an issue which does cause concern within the wider community. Like it or not, there is a popular distrust of both sets of paramilitary groupings and a strong belief that the retention of weapons is a deliberate lever to apply pressure in the negotiations. The Unionist parties' attitude to decommissioning is not, however, as genuine as that of the community. They harbor suspicion of Sinn Féin and indeed ourselves, but are driven more by a reluctance to be inclusive. They wish that a settlement could be found by the "main constitutional parties" to the exclusion of ourselves and Sinn Féin. In this respect, they are out of step with the people. Those who have contributed to the conflict must contribute to the search for a solution. This is a basic foundation for the resolution of the conflict. Indeed, it could be argued that it is because of the inability of such "constitutional parties" to deal with the situation that the conflict has continued for so long. The ordinary people understand this view.

Unionists must be honest with themselves and be prepared for the necessity of inclusive talks. They should listen to the people more closely. Their intransigence does not reflect the preparedness of the ordinary people on the ground. The conditions may not be ideal for dialogue to take place, but time is not on the side of the peace process. The only ones who have not taken any risks in this process are the Unionist parties, because they are not yet a part of the process.

The British government, too, is playing a dangerous game. They have miscalculated the decommissioning ploy, erecting it so firmly that they have gotten themselves onto an impossible hook. This cast-iron position has ensured that there will have to be an eventual climbdown by the government. They will be gutted by their own party and by Unionists for giving in to terrorists, all because they themselves have created an unachievable precondition.

Is this because they have been forced into a position through the paranoia of disunity within the party, or do they simply fail to comprehend the situation? I know that some in the Northern Ireland Office are exasperated by the lack of appreciation for their position, but what else is new? It is because successive governments have, in the past, been unable to grasp an understanding for the nuances of Ulster politics that so many blunders have been associated with Northern Ireland. Why should we expect that this government should be any less prone to such mismanagement?

I think that they do now wish to see discussions taking place, but cannot find a formula to make this happen. They cannot pressure the Unionist politicians because that will only provoke further isolation. They cannot overcome the arms issue and, because of that, they can only be minimalist in any movement which benefits the paramilitaries. This, in turn, makes movement on arms less likely, as those organizations perceive the government to be foot-dragging. Meanwhile, the Irish government is exposing them even further by moving unilaterally. The only way out is to be prepared to take risks to help move the entire situation forward.

As for the arms issue, I believe that it is the paramilitary organizations who must deal with this issue, which has become an impediment to progress, for devious purposes from some corners, but more importantly in the minds of the ordinary people. Their fears are legitimate and have to be addressed. Uncertainty of whether one side or the other will return to war because they cannot achieve their goals is an understandable concern for many people.

The Combined Loyalist Military Command issued a statement on August 25, outlining its position. It stated that they were committed to pursuing a settlement through exclusively peaceful means and that their weapons were defensive, stating that so long as the rights of the people were upheld in the peace process, there would be no first strike. They also alluded that they would be prepared to disarm if the IRA disarmed. This is an important statement. Loyalists are not the obstacles to decommissioning.

The IRA should now clarify its position. As long as uncertainty surrounds their intentions and commitment, it will be difficult to build the confidence which is essential to the pursuit of a settlement. I am not happy with the overall situation, yet I have to accept that we are where we are and, rather than apportioning blame, we have a responsibility to try to bring the peace process back on track. I feel frustrated that Unionists have hidden from the challenges they must face by erecting barriers, but I am also frustrated that Republicans are doing nothing to help break the impasse. Where is the evidence of the "critical compromises" Adams has talked about, or does he believe, as Martin McGuinness said earlier this month, that only Unionists and the British government can give? The gridlock must be overcome if the peace process is to have any hope, but everyone has a part to play in making the compromises which will make this possible.

Clinton Must Show His Even-Handedness

(*Irish Voice* November 29–December 5, 1995)

US President Bill Clinton visited Northern Ireland for the first time on November 30, 1995. Receiving a universally warm welcome, he was able to inject new life into the flagging peace process by engendering confidence in the population.

There is a great deal of anticipation here in Ulster surrounding the impending visit by President Clinton on Thursday, and what effect it will have on our wee place. The people won't know what hit them when his massive entourage descends onto Belfast. The prospect of hundreds of secret service agents roaming our streets, armed to the teeth, wearing Ray-Bans in the middle of winter and talking into their cufflinks, is bound to extract some curiosity from the natives.

It's hard to say what the expectations are in the community. I think the initial reaction will be one of bewilderment. As details are beginning to emerge about the visit, some in the media are portraying it as merely a highly charged publicity exercise designed more for consumption back home in the States than in Ireland. That is, of course, an element, but I believe the intentions of the President are sincere and that he is acting in the interest of peace.

When I was in the States two weeks ago, I clearly picked up the message from the White House that this trip was meant to have substance and was not just for public relations. This was also apparent in talking to many others who were concerned that the visit would be pointless if there wasn't political development to punctuate the importance of the event. The worrying element of this school of thought is the lack of understanding of the effects here if the President chose to cancel his trip.

There are two elements to the significance of the visit. One is what practical benefits it can create for the peace process and the economy. The second, equally important one, is the latent impact it will have upon the atmosphere in our society, especially as the community is not in an optimistic frame of mind. The serious condition of the peace process is creating despair. All that people have heard for the past year after the euphoria died down is talk of crisis and return to war; all they have seen are the negative by-products of a stumbling process. The people need to be reminded of what has been achieved and of the opportunities that lie ahead. We need an atmospheric change which will assist in providing the community with the will to go on, to overcome the present difficulties. The notion that the peace is now unwinnable must be dispelled. Imagine what terrible effect the postponement of the President's trip would have had on a society, which has already begun to lose hope. The budget crisis almost made it inevitable but, thankfully, that has been overcome.

There exists a massive potential for the President to give the process a kick-start, but not by knocking heads to force change. Let him tell us about the people who are alive, who are presently breathing peaceful air, who, if not for the ceasefires, would be dead. Let's, fingers crossed, hear news of economic investment, or US commitments to trade in Northern Ireland. About the jobs which are created here now, few as they are, that would not have come but for the ending of the Troubles, and the hope and worth they have given to those who were otherwise condemned to the dole queue. People need to feel good about the peace. There is enough bad news about the place.

President Clinton may remind us that we have created the best opportunity for peace in our land, and that we are presently squandering it. We need help and encouragement to focus minds on how we can revitalize the peace process. But here is where it becomes tricky. The line between encouragement and interference is a thin one, and one which must be carefully trodden. There are those who have sought to counsel the application of pressure against the British government or the Unionists. I have counselled at all times on my visits to the States that a balanced and even-handed approach is essential. We cannot have a situation where America is seen to be cheerleader for one side or the other. The President's responsibility is to act only in the interest of peace and the people of Northern Ireland as a whole.

Gerry Adams has promised to internationalize the problem in an attempt to force the British to back down. That is not the way forward. David Trimble helped Adams' cause significantly when he was in the States the week before us by displaying a wholly offensive attitude. I spent the entire duration of my time there fighting the fires which he had ignited. But then, what's new?

Intransigence is nothing unique to Ulster and it can and must be overcome. The US needs to maintain a clear head and not allow itself to be used by one side against the other. Remember, this peace process belongs not to Adams or Trimble or to me, but to all the people. So, a lot of people are on eggshells, waiting to see if Clinton will come here and offend someone and leave us with the mess. But I don't think that will happen.

How much will materialize from the visit remains to be seen. We will see what we will see. But at the very least, I would hope that some confidence can be instilled in the community, at this most crucial of times. Gerry Adams has said that there is now no peace process. President Clinton has the capability of helping us all believe that indeed there still is. Peace is difficult. It was always going to be that way, but it cannot be walked away from.

Part Three—1996

The year of 1996 was characterized by the decline of the Conservative government's majority and consequent dependence upon the Unionist MPs not to bring the government down. The lack of movement toward negotiations also put severe strain on both the Loyalist and Republican ceasefires. The January sidelining of the Mitchell Report in favor of elections and the changing balance of forces within Republicanism ultimately led the IRA to end its ceasefire on February 9. The Canary Wharf bombing in London was followed by a renewed IRA mainland campaign. Nevertheless, elections to all-party talks took place on May 30, with the result of Sinn Féin receiving seventeen seats and the PUP and UDP receiving two seats each. Failure to reinstate the IRA ceasefire, however, left Sinn Féin barred from the negotiations, which finally opened in June. Tension over Orange parades marked much of the summer, only to be followed by deadlock over the issue of decommissioning once the negotiations resumed. Attempts at expelling the UDP and PUP over the CLMC death-threat to Billy Wright and Alex Kerr, the emergence of the Loyalist Volunteer Force, and the return of the IRA bombing campaign to Northern Ireland with the Thiepval Barracks bombing in October, put severe strain on the Loyalist ceasefire. Thus, by the end of the year, the lack of progress in the negotiations, the crumbling Loyalist ceasefire and continuing Republican violence left the people of Northern Ireland wondering whether there was still a peace process left.

■ ■ ■

Assembly "Fantasy" Will Destroy Negotiations
(*Irish Voice* January 31–February 6, 1996)

On January 24, Prime Minister John Major, while officially accepting the Mitchell Report, stated that he could see no reason why paramilitaries should not begin decommissioning and that the government's demands for decommissioning before talks remained valid. UUP leader David Trimble welcomed Major's statement and called for elections to talks to be held in April or May.

This has undoubtedly been the craziest week I have experienced in the entire peace process. I think that everybody was shocked and caught unawares by the episodes in the House of Commons last week. The actions of the British Prime Minister John Major and the Unionist parties (led by David Trimble and Ian Paisley) were a decisive kick in the teeth for George Mitchell and his commission. Their dismissal of Mitchell's report is an insult to all right-minded people.

The UDP supported the establishment of the commission as a possible way to encourage a realistic analysis of the weapons issue, and we were willing to make submissions to the body in the hope that the impasse could be broken. I found in my dealings with them that all three of the commissioners were genuinely dedicated to investigating all the relevant aspects of this very complex issue, and I must say that I was impressed by the professional way in which they approached their task. I had said at the time that the greatest difficulty for the commission was the limited time allocated for them to deal with the given task. Indeed, I think that, under the circumstances, they produced a sensible and carefully considered document. While there was a feeling of certainty about the direction of the report, there still existed some anticipation about what reaction would be forthcoming from the various parties. A compromise position was expected and that was what the commission delivered. The question was who would accept the compromise?

There are elements in the report which may prove a challenge for one side or the other, but it is a largely sensible approach and is, in my view, a step in the right direction. The recommendation that participants in negotiations subscribe to principles as suggested in the report is something to which no democratically constituted political party could reasonably object. More controversial is the recommendation that decommissioning should take place within negotiations. The UDP has stated consistently – as have Republicans – that this issue can best be dealt with alongside other issues in the negotiations. It is a commonsense position.

We can accept that the issue must be satisfactorily dealt with and I believe that there is a determination to do so within negotiations. This concept warrants further exploration. However, there are inherent difficulties, depending on how decommissioning could actually be dealt with. It would be ridiculous to move into a process in which some parties would trade off political movement for arms. This would be an unacceptable subversion of the ethos of negotiations.

Mitchell's proposals do not in any way constitute a magic formula, but they represent a reasonable basis for further discussion, or at least they would if we could get back to that position. The opportunity offered by the Mitchell report was quickly and very effectively buried by John Major and the mainstream Unionist parties. Their calculated injection of potential elections into the debate has blown all discussion of Mitchell right out of the water. All the talk of deals for Unionist votes in Westminster has been well aired, so I won't go into it further. It is obvious that there is no innocent motivation to either Major's or the Unionists' approach but that those motivations are quite different.

Major plucked the few sentences which alluded to an elected body out of the Mitchell report and used them for his springboard, even though Mitchell stated explicitly that he was making no recommendation about such a body, merely that it was one option. Major has talked of decommissioning as a means of access to all-party talks. His position, while reprehensible, is somewhat more honest than Trimble's or Paisley's.

Trimble got to his feet less than two minutes after Major in the Commons and added an entirely more sinister spin. His proposal is that such a body would still not negotiate until decommissioning begins, it would only debate. It appears to me that he wishes to create a body which fulfils the Unionist fantasy of an assembly, while making agreement politically impossible.

I am entirely opposed to elections to a body of any form as a matter of principle. I am a democrat and my party is committed to fighting elections, but this is not the best way to proceed in the present circumstances. The Unionist parties argue that they require a fresh mandate to allow them to negotiate with Sinn Féin. This is nonsense. They cooperate with Sinn Féin on local councils around the province as it is.

I am convinced that elections will further divide the parties and destroy any negotiations process, locking the negotiators into impossible hard-line manifesto positions as they attempt to gut each other at the polls. The motivation behind the proposal is driven by a desire to achieve three things. They wish to see parties such as ours destroyed and excluded from the negotiation process. They want to create a split in the Nationalist consensus, forcing the SDLP and Sinn Féin against each other at the polls and, lastly, they want to reinforce a hard-line mandate against change.

It is sickening to me as a Unionist and a Loyalist that these people are prepared to play games with the peace process in such a cynical way. I oppose elections and will continue to oppose them. For this process to succeed, we must move into full negotiations and they must be within a framework designed to reach conclusive agreement. There needs to be a reasonable consensus among the parties as to how we proceed to negotiations and how that process will be constituted. Unionist parties are prepared to condemn everyone to elections before there is even agreement upon what people will be elected to.

The current climate is one that can be described in no other terms than irrational. Everyone is blowing the lids. What we need is for the steam to be taken out of the situation and for engagement in some rational debate about how we can agree upon a common approach toward negotiation. No one has the right to impose his or her proposals on others. An elected body of some form is an option that is a legitimate proposal for discussion – but it is no more than that.

They must decide whether they wish to sacrifice the very peace process for their "holy grail" of an assembly. The sensible way forward is to rewind to the Mitchell report and explore that. I am confident that the essence of that document can offer a sound basis upon which agreement may be reached on the structure, format and agenda for all-party negotiations. The objective now must be to get to that point.

IRA Must Be Penalized for Destroying Peace

(*Irish Voice* February 14–20, 1996)

At 6 p.m. on February 9, the IRA issued a statement ending its ceasefire, blaming the British Prime Minister and Unionist leaders "for squandering this unprecedented opportunity to resolve the conflict." At 7:01 p.m. a bomb exploded near Canary Wharf in London, killing two men, injuring more than one hundred others, and causing an estimated £85 million worth of damage.

The tragic events of last Friday evening have left me stunned and uncertain about the future. There has always been a possibility that the ceasefires could break, but it was still a shock when I learned of the bombing in London. Only the night before, I had taken part in a live television debate with Pat McGeown of Sinn Féin, the first time Loyalists and Republicans had done so. It was a step forward, albeit a small one. There was a tremendously positive public response about the show. Today, that positive feeling is gone.

I have never experienced such despondency in the community, even at the height of the Troubles. They feel that something has been stolen from them, something they were just learning to appreciate. The opportunity afforded them almost eighteen months ago was the hope of peace, something they had not experienced for twenty-five years. Now that hope is disappearing. As the dust settles, the question on people's lips is "What now?" The country is collectively holding its breath to see what direction the IRA may take. That shall have a tremendous influence upon how others react.

One must, however, be reminded that before Friday there were two ceasefires; now one remains. The Loyalist paramilitaries who initiated their cessation of hostilities in October 1994 must now consider their position. It was stated by the Combined Loyalist Military Command (CLMC) in August of last year that they would not initiate a return to war, that there would be "no first strike." The IRA has now made such a proactive move.

The Loyalist organizations have demonstrated remarkable restraint so far in these difficult circumstances. The CLMC has been unquestionably committed throughout this peace process to achieving a democratic resolution of the conflict and remains so; however, it is compelled to defend its community from attack. The responsibility of avoiding a return to war lies squarely at the feet of the IRA. I, along with my party, am fully committed to finding a peaceful way forward and averting further conflict. I believe that much will depend upon the actions of Republicans in coming days and weeks, and I have no doubt that Loyalists will be keeping the evolving situation under constant review.

The IRA has excluded itself from the democratic process by its initiation of violence, and the penalties for walking away from peace must be demonstrated. Sinn Féin has maintained its prominent position because it represents the IRA in this process, yet Gerry Adams has illustrated that he has been unable to retain influence and control. Doors were opened to Gerry Adams because he brought the IRA into the peace process but, now that the organization has walked away from peace, those doors must be closed. The IRA cannot have its cake and eat it. I believe it is imperative that President Clinton demonstrate his rejection of the IRA's position by reversing the concessions he made. Sinn Féin's funds in the US must be frozen, and the visas granted for Adams and others must be revoked. They must be shown that craziness is the wrong way.

On the number of times when I came to the States to offer my message when other Unionists would not, I found the Irish American community in New York to be good-hearted and warm, genuinely committed to building peace in Ireland and willing to hear what I had to say, even though they did not share my view. I believe I have learned and grown from my experiences here, and it is because of this that I appeal now through this column to those with influence to help salvage this desperate situation. The IRA and Sinn Féin must be convinced by the Irish people that they have embarked upon the wrong course. This cannot be the way forward. I do not believe that any of us want to fight another war. How many more people will have to die before we realize that it cannot succeed?

Blame has been laid for Friday's bomb, but there can be no justification for a return to war. The IRA must be encouraged to stop this thing before it becomes uncontrollable, before it is too late, before there is no escape. I find it difficult to comprehend what the IRA hopes to achieve by returning to conflict. There are no logical explanations for lifting the ceasefire. There is no support within the Catholic community for a return to violence. I believe that all right-minded people must say clearly and firmly that there is no support for the IRA's actions, and seek to convince the IRA to reinstate its ceasefire. The peace process must continue, with or without the IRA, and all efforts must be made to achieve all-party negotiations. Sinn Féin cannot be accepted within that process if it is prepared to support a dual strategy. The days of the ballot box and the armalite have gone.

We have to focus our minds on how, in these difficult times, we can retrieve the situation and move forward. Ulster Unionist Party leader David Trimble still holds firm that there should be elections, but there is no consensus upon what body those elections should be to. I oppose elections. The potential further division which would promise at this delicate juncture should be avoided at all costs and I would urge that we respect the immediacy of the need to regain control of the peace process.

I suggest that the best way forward now is for parties to enter a negotiation framework based upon the democratic principles proposed by the Mitchell Commission. To gain entry into those negotiations, Republicans would be required to resume their ceasefire and accept the Mitchell Principles. Their position within any form of negotiations is meaningless if there is a threat or use of force or if they cannot accept the outcome of those negotiations. The IRA must decide once and for all whether it is prepared for war or for peace. It cannot be afforded a half-way house. That decision must be made soon, before the opportunity is lost forever.

IRA Ceasefire a Prerequisite for Talks
(*Irish Voice* March 20–26, 1996)

The annual St. Patrick's Day reception at the White House was overshadowed by the breakdown of the IRA ceasefire and frantic attempts behind the scenes to get the Republican movement back on board.

This St. Patrick's week has been an interesting departure from last year's festivities. As I watched the goings-on in the States, I couldn't help chuckling at the differences a year could make. Last year, Sinn Féin leader Gerry Adams was given the key to the White House – this year they changed the locks. Last year, the Unionist party refused to take part and, this time around, party leader David Trimble was there; the party faithful applauded his courage for being the first Unionist to go. I couldn't help wondering if I had imagined being at the White House last year and the lambasting I had taken from the Unionist Party for taking up the President's invitation. Changed times. This year I wasn't there, thinking it prudent to keep attention on things at home at this difficult time. But I didn't miss the ironies even from this distance. The Taoiseach John Bruton appeared to be offending Irish Americans even more capably than David Trimble, and that's saying something. I wish I had been there to see it all.

But all joking aside, this is a very serious time and, for some, the last week or so in the States will have been an important one. And for none more so than Adams. This is, of course, the first opportunity for him to appraise the effects that the IRA's return to war have had in this vital constituency. I think the message he returns with will be of vital importance.

I have been watching and listening carefully. I can understand the desire of Irish America not to cold-shoulder Gerry Adams and I certainly would not have imagined that he would have been shunned. But behind the smiles at the glittering functions and the parade in New York, I detected a message to the IRA that things could not be the same for them. A positive signal for Loyalists was the remark by Mutual of America chairman Bill Flynn that the IRA must reinstate its ceasefire with "no ifs and buts." It is crucial that Adams should clearly understand that there is no tolerance for a continuation of the conflict and that this is firmly relayed to the IRA.

There is no justification for the IRA to continue its campaign and there is no evident logic in its position. I find it difficult to understand its strategy at this time. Surely, the IRA cannot actually believe that its position will be advanced by murdering more people? There exists no firm indication of the rationale behind its refusal to reinstate its ceasefire. The closest I can come is a demand that there be no preconditions to all-party negotiations. Sinn Féin chairman Mitchel McLaughlin said at the weekend that all issues should be addressed "without preconditions, without vetoes and with no outcome either predetermined or precluded." I certainly cannot disagree with such sentiments, but I also cannot help wondering whether he is actually saying that Sinn Féin considers the demand for an IRA ceasefire to be a precondition.

Negotiations cannot take place with one participant playing to different rules than everyone else. An IRA ceasefire is not a precondition, it is a prerequisite. If moves were made to bring Sinn Féin to the negotiating table while the IRA was continuing to kill and bomb, the peace process would disintegrate entirely. The IRA must make its mind up soon whether it is prepared to enter this process again, for time and patience are running out.

Perhaps the IRA believes that a price must be paid for its ceasefire, but what reasonable price could be demanded or should be made for a commitment to stop terrorist activity? Should the IRA be offered a greater influence in negotiations than others or is it asking for a political concession? Would that not in itself be a precondition that the IRA was setting? Clearly, the IRA must accept that it can only enter talks on the same basis as everyone else.

I fear that the truth of the matter may be that the breakdown of the ceasefire and the failure to restore it is the result of the failure of the Republican movement to come to terms with the consequences of its own arguments. The challenge for Republicans has been to face up to the reality that they are unlikely to achieve their political objectives through democratic means alone. I believe that the debate which has been taking place internally has not produced an acceptance that the pursued objective of a united Ireland should be placed at the mercy of the democratic procedure.

This has been demonstrated by their failure to sign up to the principle of consent in the Forum for Peace and Reconciliation, thus breaking the Nationalist consensus. This fundamental democratic parameter is accepted not only by every other Nationalist party in Ireland but by every other party in the British Isles, and is supported by the US administration. This is indicative of the inflexibility of the IRA's political position.

The IRA shall have to commit itself to either end or continue the campaign very soon. The Sinn Féin *Árd Fheis* (annual party conference) this weekend should provide the first indication of what direction it is going in. There is no room for the ballot box and the armalite – it can only be one or the other. The date has been set for the all-party negotiations and the opportunity is there for Sinn Féin to take its place alongside all others – if the IRA allows it to.

The Combined Loyalist Military Command stated last week that the IRA's campaign could not be allowed to continue without a "telling response." It also urged the IRA to "bring us back from the brink." I have no doubts that Loyalists desire the peace process to continue, yet there is an absolute commitment to defend the community from Republican attacks. It is essential that Republicans understand fully the consequences of a full-scale resumption of conflict and avoid such a scenario. Such a war would merely inflict further intolerable suffering upon a community which has already suffered enough, particularly the working-class people in both communities who have borne the brunt of the conflict.

Turning Point for Peace Process
(*Irish Voice* May 29–June 4, 1996)

Elections to all-party talks were scheduled for May 30, almost two years after the peace process was initiated with the 1994 ceasefires. In an attempt to make the negotiations as inclusive as possible, an electoral system with a top-up provision benefiting smaller parties was devised.

The election which takes place in Northern Ireland on Thursday represents a turning point for the peace process. It signals the step over the threshold into negotiations. For almost two years we have been trying to get to the point where negotiations could take place. It has been a difficult road, almost costing the entire peace process. It is unfortunate that the route to these talks has been by way of an election. Elections are divisive and will send parties to negotiations with exaggerated mandate positions. It also risks the exclusion of key players, and therefore it actually counters the ethos of this peace process. Parties such as mine have a contribution to make to the negotiations and the process as a whole, which cannot be accurately measured by votes alone. Yet I am confident that we shall do well in the election and that we will be there on June 10 to negotiate.

Another unfortunate and, under the circumstances, untimely aspect of this election is that it has given opportunity to Sinn Féin to hide behind a renewed electoral mandate as a shield against facing its responsibilities at this time. Gerry Adams demands that his party should be allowed entry into the all-party talks on the sole basis of its mandate. He is clearly distorting the truth of this situation. Like us, Sinn Féin's contribution to the peace process cannot be measured solely by electoral strength. It represents the voice of the IRA and, as such, it is bound in many ways by the actions of the IRA. It is entirely proper that Sinn Féin should be excluded from the talks while the IRA is engaged in a terrorist campaign for "in order to have the best opportunity for success the talks should take place in a peaceful environment." – Martin McGuinness' words, not mine.

All participants in the negotiations should be expected to abide by the same set of rules. If Sinn Féin was to be allowed entry into negotiations while the IRA ceasefire had not been restored, then I can assure you that the party would find itself alone at the table. Sinn Féin argues that there should be no pre-conditions, that no outcome be predetermined or precluded. But the reinstatement of the ceasefire is not a precondition and should not be considered one. Nor should the indication, which I welcome, from Gerry Adams that Sinn Féin is prepared to accept the Mitchell Principles be viewed as a substitute for a ceasefire. The passport to negotiations is there if Sinn Féin wishes to take it. If it refuses to come back into the peace process, then we must move on without it. That is not ideal but it is the only option.

The other major element, which has yet to be fully addressed, is how the negotiations shall proceed. It is clear that some wish to avert real progress in talks and that there is an unwillingness to engage. It is vital that those who participate in talks display a determination to make the process succeed. I, for one, can commit the Ulster Democratic Party to full, open and honest dialogue and a firm determination to reach a fair and just political settlement. I believe it is our duty to take these negotiations seriously, as it is in all probability the last bastion from an all-out return to war. The alternative to a settlement is the domination of one community by the other as a result of conflict. That, of course, is not the way forward.

Some Republicans argue that there is no point in negotiating because the Unionists will dig in their heels at every turn and there will be no equity. In return, some Unionists would argue that there is no point because Republicans are so transfixed on a united Ireland that they will resort to violence again anyway if they don't get their way. Canary Wharf did little to help diffuse that perception. I am fed up hearing the "whingers" from both sides crying about demands and guarantees and promises. It's time to get there and make it happen, with everyone on the same level playing field. No inbuilt advantages.

I am convinced that the talks will develop a dynamic of their own. There is no room for any one issue to become an obstacle to overall progress, nor should issues be ignored. We must ensure that it simply does not happen. I certainly hope that the positions of those who seek to subvert or avoid progress will be unsustainable in the company of all others who have the determination to push forward regardless. One thing is certain. We must enter the talks on June 10 and try to make them work, and it definitely won't work if we don't go in to try. Only time will tell.

What More Does the IRA Want?

(*Irish Voice* June 26–July 2, 1996)

On May 30, Sinn Féin received 15.5 percent of the total votes in the Forum elections. Having campaigned on the basis of "A vote for Sinn Féin is a vote for Peace," the party received its highest electoral share since the beginning of the Troubles. On June 15, the IRA detonated a 1.5 tonne car bomb in the center of Manchester, injuring two hundred people and causing an estimated £100 million worth of damage.

The IRA bombing of Manchester has dealt the peace process a savage blow. It was the first demonstration of how the IRA has chosen to interpret the increased Republican vote in the recent election. Some commentators at the time viewed the 118,000 votes as a mandate for peace. That was naïve. Many people gave their support to Sinn Féin in the belief that it would give Gerry Adams a strong hand for arguing for a renewed ceasefire. But why they received the mandate is not important. I pointed out at the time that the central issue was how Sinn Féin and the IRA chose to apply it.

Our worst fears were realized in Manchester, when the IRA used the Republican mandate as a validation of their twin military/political strategy. This is confirmed by Adams' refusal to condemn the Manchester bomb. He insisted that Sinn Féin should be allowed entry to talks regardless of what the IRA did. This, of course, is nonsense. If Sinn Féin is holding out for a forced entry into talks, then it will have a long wait.

There is no logic to the Republican position. They argue that an IRA ceasefire is a precondition and should be dropped. So, in order to convince others that the need for a ceasefire and decommissioning should be removed, they explode a massive bomb in a crowded city center injuring over two hundred civilians. That should do it! The IRA is rapidly painting itself into a corner. Its actions are hardening attitudes toward Republicans, causing even their strongest supporters to lose patience.

Their position internationally is being discredited. Time is starting to run out for the Provos; the crunch point is quickly approaching. The variables around which the prospect of a ceasefire revolved are no longer variables. Irish Foreign Minister Dick Spring expressed his consternation when he let loose that all that they had asked for was there, George Mitchell being the final element. Clearly, there is nothing more to hold out for, so they will soon have to make a decision.

Either the IRA is going to be forced to cut its losses and call a ceasefire, giving it entry into the negotiations in a weaker state than before Canary Wharf and facing an uphill struggle to gain credibility, or it may decide that to enter talks in the present circumstances is to suffer humiliation. In that case, it will probably opt to do what it knows best and re-engage a full military campaign. It is even possible that Republicans believe that the process has been contorted to a point where it is possible for them to engage from a stronger position. Adams and others, in my opinion, may view this to be the case. Indeed, an understanding of the Republican psyche would suggest that the best way forward is for the IRA to destroy the present process, or preferably prompt it to self-destruct, then work toward an eventual re-genesis driven by a sustained war campaign. Such a full circle could conceivably be achieved in seven to ten years.

This is a very depressing scenario. However, it is not far-fetched. It is the view of the Ulster Freedom Fighters, a group which is on ceasefire, that an IRA campaign in Northern Ireland is imminent, and the UFF have publicly stated that their personnel have been placed on alert accordingly. They have said that they "are prepared for all eventualities."

There must be no doubt that the peace process has reached a critical point. In my view, we have reached the edge of the abyss, and it may take very little to cast us into its depths. But the opportunity still exists for the peace process to be saved. The IRA has the power to de-escalate the situation by an immediate re-instatement of its ceasefire. The question is – humiliation or not – are Republicans prepared to accept the responsibility for the so many deaths that further conflict promises? The choice is theirs.

I, along with my colleagues, will do everything in my power to avert the disintegration of the peace process, but much lies in the hands of the IRA. There is no logical reason not to re-instate the ceasefire, only a cynical and selfish one. The negotiations are ongoing, and Republicans have entry. Senator Mitchell is in the chair, which was a crucial factor in Republican thinking. What more can they reasonably expect? It's make up your mind time. I hope they make the right choice.

Sinn Féin Deserves No More US Support

(*Irish Voice* July 3-9, 1996)

On June 28, mortars were fired from a parked car at a British army barracks in Osnabrück, Germany. While roofs and facades of buildings were damaged, there were no injuries. The attack was later claimed by the IRA and was reminiscent of attacks in the 1980s in which the IRA targeted British Army installations on the European mainland since they were considered to be less fortified. The Osnabrück bombing sparked fears of a new IRA campaign against British targets in Europe.

The peace process has suffered another blow in the past week, which must force us to re-examine the potential for a return to democratic methods by Republicans. It looks like they are moving in entirely the opposite direction. The IRA mortar attack on a British army installation in Osnabrück, Germany, signals a significant departure from the Provo strategy since the Canary Wharf bombing. In so far as their campaign has been carried out to date, it has been confined to the British mainland and against economic rather than military targets. The fact that they have now applied themselves to internationalizing their campaign raises questions, or perhaps answers some existing ones, in relation to the intentions of the IRA.

While some still hope that Republicans will come back into the democratic process, one has to wonder whether there is any inclination within the Republican movement toward restoring the ceasefire. One could lend oneself to the belief that the actions of the IRA post-Canary Wharf very much resembled treading water. That the Republican movement was somehow going through the motions, flexing its muscles but still open to being convinced to return to the peace process, that, in their words, the process from their perspective "could be rebuilt."

I wanted to believe this myself, and I must confess I still want to believe it. But recent events suggest that the IRA is neither treading water, nor is it wrestling with itself.

Manchester represented an escalation of activity in mainland Britain, and now Osnabrück widens the campaign. It looks very likely that the Provos are moving in a very definite direction, and in a calculated way.

One would suspect that a great deal of effort is required logistically to plan, prepare, and execute an attack such as that in Osnabrück. I would conclude that this attack leads from a direct decision by the IRA's Army Council to broaden its sphere of operation, and that such a decision is strategic. While it could be thought that it is in some part a demonstration of strength, an indication of its reach, this is no act of symbolism. Such reach is not effortlessly achieved. The IRA will not have put so much time and so many resources into this operation solely to achieve Osnabrück.

The IRA, in my view, has taken a deliberate and conscious decision to extend its campaign to another level and, as such, I must believe that it expects to follow it through to its conclusion. The actions of the IRA effectively dash any hopes it is still interested in peace. The timing of the bombing, coming only days after President Clinton vowed a strong stance against international terrorism, speaks volumes about how weighty the President's opinion is with the IRA. It has shown a consistent disregard for the views of all others, following its own selfish and cynical agenda fanatically.

I have listened to those in America, and in the Republic of Ireland, and in Northern Ireland, who argue that they must keep the door open for Sinn Féin while there is any hope that it can be convinced to come back into the peace process. I have understood that view, even if I did not agree. Surely such patience cannot be inexhaustible. Those who continue to hold the door ajar for Republicans must by now be asking themselves why should they bother, when every step which is taken to help them is responded to by a slap in the face. I believe it is time for Sinn Féin to be shown that there can be no help for those who refuse to help themselves.

I have written to the White House to make my views known. I have asked that action be put behind President Clinton's words, and that measures be taken to curb the ability of the IRA and Sinn Féin to fundraise and propagandize in the United States. Republicans must be shown very clearly that there is no reward for violence, that the rewards lie in the democratic process.

Negotiations are currently under way in Belfast. These talks offer a clear opportunity for a peaceful settlement to be reached through dialogue. That is the only legitimate way forward. There is no future in war. If Republicans really wanted peace, they would reinstate their ceasefire and take their place in those talks. By not doing so and by continuing to execute their campaign of terror, they are turning their backs on all the people in Ireland, in Britain, and throughout the world who want to see peace in our country.

Now Is the Time to Pull Back
(*Irish Voice* July 17–23, 1996)

On July 6, the RUC announced its decision to re-route the following day's Drumcree Orange parade away from the Garvaghy Road. Seeing this decision as a threat to Protestant culture and identity as well as an attempt to appease Republicans, the Orange Order refused to accept this decision. After three days of a stand-off between Orangemen and the RUC and army, accompanied by province-wide Loyalist rioting and the LVF murder of Catholic taxi driver Michael McGoldrick on July 8, the RUC reversed its decision and allowed the parade down the Garvaghy Road on July 11. The inevitable reaction was Nationalist rioting, followed by the Republican bombing of the Killyhevlin Hotel in Enniskillen.

The events of the past week or so have left our country teetering on the edge of the abyss. The question now is whether we can pull back again, or shall we be cast into its depths? I am afraid the jury is still out on that one. When the RUC Chief Constable Hugh Annesley made his fatal decision to re-route the Drumcree Church parade, he set in motion a chain of events which must bring into question his position as head of the RUC. In my view, he bears a very heavy responsibility for what transpired.

Nationalists have argued that he bowed to the rule of the mob when he finally reversed his decision on July 11. The fact of the matter is that he made the wrong decision in the first instance precisely because of the threat of Republican violence if the parade was allowed down the Garvaghy Road. Brendan McKenna of the local residents' coalition made it very clear that no compromise was acceptable, and that the RUC knew very well what the consequences would be.

Annesley capitulated to Republicans when he must have been well aware of the potential for Loyalist disorder. I find it very difficult to conceive how he could have weighed the threat of public disorder from either side and concluded in operational terms that the correct decision was to re-route the parade. I think it is closer to the truth that his initial decision was a political one, inspired by Anglo-Irish pressure. His subsequent reversal was a final acceptance of the reality of the consequences of that decision.

The scenes of last week could well have been avoided but for Hugh Annesley making the wrong call. Once he had done so, the deterioration of the overall situation with the Loyalist and then Republican violence that ensued was inevitable. The result is that Nationalists, the traditional critics of the police and the government, have now been joined by Loyalists, who have lost faith in law and order.

I found it almost laughable when I heard Brendan McKenna describe the RUC as the paramilitary wing of the Orange Order. I had spent the preceding few days hearing one horror story after another about police brutality against the Loyalists, whom McKenna suggests they were protecting.

I found police batons charging women and children. Attacking men at a peaceful protest in Antrim; beating an elderly man, then putting him in the boot of a police car. Firing baton rounds at close quarters inside a public house in East Belfast. Attacking people trying to protect their cars and property from rioters. Shooting a man in a telephone box with a plastic bullet. The list goes on. Confidence has been lost in the RUC, and that will take considerable time to restore.

The anger and frustration felt by the Loyalist community has now been deepened by the Republican bomb attack in Enniskillen. This was a further hammer blow to the peace process. The IRA's claim that it is not responsible is of little consequence. The fact that there are Republicans in possession of the skills, resources and determination to cause conflict and to attack gives severe concern to the Loyalist community, regardless of what they may choose to call themselves.

It is my view that the Killyhevlin bomb is the most serious development since the break of the IRA ceasefire. It signals that we may be on the verge of a resumption of war in Northern Ireland. Events in Enniskillen could be a turning point in our history just as they were so tragically in 1987. It is up to everyone in a leadership role to make every effort to avert a further deterioration of the situation. I can assure you that I, along with my colleagues, will be relentless in our endeavors to maintain restraint, and to give leadership to our people. It must, however, be pointed out that the government has the responsibility for the protection and well-being of its citizens. If the government is unwilling or incapable of protecting our community from Republican attack, then history tells us that the community may determine that it must defend itself.

Republicans should consider the implications of a return to conflict. Consider the intolerable suffering that war inflicts upon the people of Northern Ireland and elsewhere. It is clear that the people in our country do not desire further conflict, that they strongly long for peace. This peace can only be achieved through dialogue. Now is the time for Republicans to end their campaign of violence and to pursue a democratic resolution of the conflict. We have looked into the jaws of hell once again, but now is the time to pull back.

Republicans Want to Kill Peace Process

(*Irish Voice* September 25–October 1, 1996)

On September 23, British police and security services uncovered a large quantity of weapons in London, Sussex and South Yorkshire. In North London alone, ten tonnes of explosives and bomb-making equipment, firearms and timers were found. It was estimated that the total amount would have been sufficient to plant five bombs the size of those used in Manchester and Canary Wharf.

Monday's huge weapons and explosives find in London signifies once again that the recent optimism in some circles that an IRA ceasefire was likely was way off the mark, and raises serious questions about the intentions of Republicans. I find it amazing that such speculation emerged at all and even more so that it emerged from the source it did.

Rumors abounded the other week when Taoiseach John Bruton suggested, while in Washington, that a new ceasefire was imminent. I couldn't help wonder at this for there was clearly no evidence to support such a claim. Indeed, all evidence pointed to the contrary. SDLP leader John Hume was almost instantly on the airwaves to dispel such thoughts, followed closely by Sinn Féin's Gerry Adams. I remember remarking at the time that, if the IRA was contemplating such an option, the last person it would float the option with would be John Bruton. Moreover, if the possibility of a ceasefire had existed, it had now been dashed for the time being.

The US delegation headed by former Congressman Bruce Morrison, which came to Northern Ireland last week, was surrounded by further speculation on the back of Bruton's comments, which I am sure was unhelpful to their efforts. It was very quickly clear in the aftermath of their meetings with Sinn Féin that there was little to be optimistic about. The current in Sinn Féin appears to be that there is no future in the present talks process and that there must be a new start. When Gerry Adams speaks about rebuilding the peace process, he is talking about destroying the present one. The activities of the IRA support the conclusion that the intention of Republicans is not to enter the multi-party negotiations which are currently under way under any circumstances, but to allow this process to shake itself apart and start again anew.

I think there are two factors to support this argument. Firstly, there is absolutely no faith amongst Republicans in the present talks. The format within which the negotiations are taking place is not suitable to them. They have laid down political conditions for the consideration of a ceasefire, which by their nature are unattainable. Secondly, the IRA could not stand the internal fall-out from a decision to reinstate the ceasefire. I believe views are so strong that there would be an inevitable split within their ranks. It is widely believed that the prospect of an imminent split was the deciding factor which led to the breakdown of the Provo ceasefire in February. Once again, the IRA may deny the people peace in the interest of its own internal stability.

Sinn Féin's political demands generally go unchallenged by the media and serious commentators, despite the deeply fascistic overtones of its position. It wants negotiations on its terms only. All right-minded people would, I am sure, acknowledge that the Northern Ireland problem can only be settled through a process of dialogue and negotiation in a peaceful environment. However, while Republicans insist there must be no preconditions, they seem quite apt at providing a good few of their own.

If negotiations are to have any credible status, there must be a level playing field for everyone – as Sinn Féin has said, no outcome should be precluded or predetermined. Yet, curiously, we are told that Sinn Féin would not be in a position to recommend to the IRA that there should be a cessation, which would create that necessary peaceful environment, unless a set of conditions are in place.

Sinn Féin objects to the issue of decommissioning being prominent on the agenda for negotiation, indeed to it being there at all. It argues that there must be an agreed time-frame. It insists that there must be the prospect for real change. If no outcome is to be precluded or predetermined, how can one build a talks process which guarantees any specified measure of change? Indeed, what quantifies change in the Republican view? De-partition? Are Republicans saying that unless they know what direction these talks are going to go in and what the result may be, they won't buy into it? Is that a fair position? Would it be any less absurd if the shoe was on the other foot, for Unionists to insist that there can be no talks unless it is guaranteed that there can be no change? What the outcome of the negotiations will be can only be defined by what agreement is reached by the participants and endorsed through referendum; that cannot be predicted.

Republicans demand that there must be an agreed time-frame. This is a deliberately vague reference to the historical notion that there must be a declaration of British withdrawal within an agreed time-frame before negotiation could take place. That position is a cornerstone of IRA policy, and has been for the duration of the Troubles. It was reiterated by Sinn Féin in its policy document "Towards a Lasting Peace" and stated during the period of the recent IRA ceasefire by Martin McGuinness. Is this a realistic demand? That, while no outcome should be predetermined or precluded, the British must agree to withdraw before negotiations can happen? Hypocritical? Perhaps Republicans still suggest, as outlined in policy documents, that, when this happens, Ulster Protestants shall be offered repatriation grants to move to England to live there if they don't like the new Ireland.

It is not realistic to demand that decommissioning should be precluded from the negotiation process. No matter of importance to any participant should be excluded, nor should debate be smothered. Neither should any one issue become an obstacle to overall progress in the negotiations. I am, of course, deeply uncomfortable with the nonsensical demands from some Unionist parties that decommissioning must be addressed before negotiations on substantive issues can proceed. I am, however, prepared to listen to the views of others.

The UDP shall continue to argue that this should be examined alongside all other issues in the talks, not before. The outcome of that debate has not been determined yet but, as a participant in these talks, I know that the debate will be influenced by my party's arguments. I am here to make sure that happens and that agreement can only be reached on this issue through unanimity or sufficient consensus among the participants. Sinn Féin, on the other hand, cannot influence the manner in which this or any other issue is to be dealt with throughout these negotiations as it chose to exclude itself from the talks process. It cannot affect such issues from the outside.

The Stormont Talks are the only show in town, and Republicans must come to terms with the reality that they will have to play their part and accept a place within these negotiations on the same basis as other parties. There is no justification for continuing a terrorist campaign. Violence cannot achieve the political conditions they demand, and promises to lead us toward full-scale conflict. But then I said at the start, as evidence indicates, that may be the idea.

Remembering War as the North Waits

(*Irish Voice* November 13-19, 1996)

On June 28, 1914, the assassination of the heir-apparent to the Austro-Hungarian throne at Sarajevo set in motion the events leading up to the First World War. On August 1, Germany declared war on Russia; the Great War had begun. On May 8, 1915, the 36th Ulster Division left Northern Ireland to make its contribution to the war effort. On July 1, 1916, the Battle of the Somme began. In the first two days alone, 5,500 men of the Ulster Division had been killed or wounded.

On the closest Sunday to November 11 each year, thousands of people in Northern Ireland pay homage to the dead of the two world wars and other conflicts. I would normally be at the cenotaph in Lisburn in County Antrim to remember those from my home town who have fought and died in defense of the free world. But this year was different for me. I had the privilege to travel, along with fifty others, to the Somme in France to pay my respects on the ground where so many young men died in the Great War. That in itself was a special occasion for me, but I was even more honored to be there in the company I was with and by the reason for bringing us together.

The pilgrimage to the Somme was organized by Paddy Harte, who is a TD from Donegal, and Glenn Barr, a Loyalist community worker from Londonderry. They brought to France people from Northern Ireland and the Republic of Ireland, from the political arena, community workers, sports personalities and representatives from all the churches in the spirit of reconciliation, to share the common experience of our loss.

Remarkably, it is the first time such a trip has taken place. Until recently, the government of the Republic of Ireland refused to recognize the remembrance for those from Ireland who died on the battlefields of France. In Northern Ireland, it is mostly Protestants who attend the memorial services and there are divisions over the wearing of the poppy, the traditional symbol of remembrance, elevating it into a political issue and sectarianizing it, as happens to many things in my country.

But why should this be so? In 1914, with the start of the Great War, young men in their hundreds of thousands volunteered to fight with the allied forces against the German and Italian armies. They were told that it was the war to end all wars and they signed up to play their part. There was no conscription in Ireland, unlike Great Britain. Yet some 350,000 volunteered for duty. Young men of fourteen and fifteen years lied about their age in order to join and went to fight in a land they were unfamiliar with against an enemy whom they did not know. Those men may have come from Belfast or Dublin, Cork or Carrickfergus, Londonderry or Laois; they might have been Protestant or Catholic but, despite the deep political turmoil Ireland found itself in at that time, they fought shoulder to shoulder at the Somme against the common enemy. It is a part of history that we share and we should remember solemnly the cost in young lives.

The Battle of the Somme was the biggest offensive of the war, fought along a massive front line. The 36th Ulster Division stood at Thiepval while the 16th Irish Division fought at Guillemont. Both lost heavily. The 36th Ulster Division had five and a half thousand dead and wounded after the two days' fighting. All in all, more than three-quarters of a million people died in that war. We went to the memorial sites of the 36th and 16th Divisions on Monday, and we held a service of remembrance at each memorial to pay tribute to our countrymen who never came home after the war. Everyone wore their poppy and did so with equal pride. I stood behind Garret FitzGerald in the church. There was no sectarianism on Monday.

The purpose of this gathering was not just to draw attention to the commonality of the shared loss of World War I. I suspect it was perhaps to draw a parallel with the present "Troubles." Later in the day, we visited the Tyn-Cot memorial at the French/Belgian border and learnt that the column upon column of white headstones before us amounted to eleven thousand dead, making it the largest single burial ground for the war dead on the western front. It occurred to me that I was subconsciously drawing an imaginary line a third across the symmetrical volume of headstones, and thinking that was about how many had been killed in the Troubles. It was a poignant moment. Here was I, standing in a single graveyard where three times more people lay than were killed in the entire duration of the conflict in Ulster. It puts things in perspective to consider the enormity of the human carnage which took place even in that one spot.

I found the trip to be a memorable one. It was one which I am sure gave everyone there cause for reflection. You would have to be inhuman not to be emotionally touched by the experience we shared in France this week, to contemplate the effects of man's inhumanity to his fellow man. I couldn't help thinking that we have a heavy responsibility at this moment in time in our own land. As Northern Ireland is drawing closer and closer to a resumption of conflict, one must consider the consequences of further war. If the IRA continues to execute its murderous campaign, war becomes an inevitability. If Loyalists are forced to respond to the Republican threat, how difficult will it be to break the spiral of conflict once again? Will it ever be so?

The opportunity, small as it is, still exists to pull back from the brink, for our political differences to be resolved through dialogue. For groups to pursue political objectives by democratic means, not violent aggression. The IRA has the power to avert war if it is its will. If it does not, then it condemns the people of Ireland, North and South, to endure further intolerable suffering.

Republicanism claims to pursue the unification of Catholic, Protestant and dissenter, but what the IRA promises is the opposite. The only unity I saw this week was that of Catholic, Protestant and dissenter lying side by side in their thousands in France. Will the IRA not be happy until the graveyards in Ireland eclipse the grotesque grandeur of Tyn-Cot?

IRA Must Adopt "No First Strike" Policy
(*Irish Voice* November 27–December 3, 1996)

On November 15, Sinn Féin's Martin McGuinness outlined the steps for the British government to achieve a re-establishment of the IRA ceasefire. He called for assurances that there would be a "credible process of talks, without pre-conditions, on a broadly acceptable time-frame and with which everyone can engage in initiatives to build confidence."

There has been intense speculation over the past week that there will soon be a decision in relation to an IRA ceasefire. A Sinn Féin meeting in Meath last Saturday is understood to have been a forum for IRA delegates also, and designed to gauge support for the current strategy.

British Prime Minister John Major has been presented with a set of proposals from SDLP leader John Hume and Sinn Féin leader Gerry Adams, which he is actively considering. The proposals appear to be the terms for what Republicans require to facilitate another IRA ceasefire. It seems clear that we are rapidly approaching the crunch point. Decisions are likely to be made this week which will have a profound effect upon the direction of the peace process, or, indeed on whether it will survive at all.

Sinn Féin's Mitchel McLaughlin said on Monday that, if John Major rejects the demands, it will be a "fatal miscalculation." Ominous words indeed. So let us consider what these proposals are. They have not been published, but there is some understanding of what they are alleged to contain:

- A guarantee of immediate inclusion of Sinn Féin in the negotiations.
- No preconditions – in other words, the removal of decommissioning from the agenda.
- An agreed time-frame for the duration of the negotiations.
- Confidence-building measures.

The first demand, which relates to Sinn Féin's inclusion in negotiations, is somewhat misjudged. It may be up to the government to determine whether Sinn Féin should be invited to participate in the negotiating process, as was the case with all other parties. However, it is up to the participants to decide whether they are prepared to accept the participation of another delegation, and the government is obliged to take account of this. Therefore, Republicans have a responsibility to convince others that they are serious, especially since they face a credibility problem following the breakdown of the IRA ceasefire. Otherwise, there may be rows of empty seats at the talks table.

In relation to the removal of the decommissioning issue from the agenda of the negotiations, the government does not have the power to make unilateral decisions about the content of the talks agenda. It is the body of all those who participate in the negotiations which holds a corporate ownership of its management. In other words, it is not the government which must be convinced one way or the other about how decommissioning is addressed, it is the other participants, particularly those who are proponents. We, as Loyalists, who are equally opposed to decommissioning, have had to meet this challenge within the talks process so far. If Republicans believe that they can contort the agreed matters of business within the talks over the heads of the participants, they are naïve indeed.

In terms of the need for an agreed time-frame for negotiations, I make the point that one does exist. When the talks were launched, it was made clear that they would work to a timetable of twelve months, with a potential extension of up to a further twelve months, if required, to find agreement. That is, in my view, a realistic timetable, for we are now already six months down the line and we have not entered substantive negotiations yet. It is unlikely that matters as complex as those we face in Northern Ireland can be resolved in a few months, but there must also be a reasonable limit in order that the participants are compelled by the time-frame in a practical sense to strive for agreement.

It is possible, of course, that the rationale behind the demand on this issue is that negotiations cannot actually be determined to have begun until Sinn Féin is at the table and therefore the stop-watch would have to be reset. That is, of course, unacceptable. What has been agreed thus far between the participants who have been engaged in negotiation since June cannot be re-negotiated and the time passed cannot be erased to facilitate Republican entry into the process.

Lastly – confidence-building measures. It is unclear exactly what Republicans are referring to here, but it is reasonable to expect that they mean police reform, action against Orange parades, removal of troops from Northern Ireland and other matters of this ilk. I hope there will be positive changes, particularly in relation to security levels, but that is something which can only happen as part of the natural normalization process which is, of course, related to the levels of terrorist threat at a given time.

The first fundamental observation which must be made about the proposals upon which we are told the peace process depends is that these are proposals which cover only one side of the equation. There is no attempt to suggest that any conditions will be met with regard to the terms of a new ceasefire. Sinn Féin continually declares that there is no point going to the IRA for a ceasefire unless the government can give assurances that the same thing will not happen again. But, for those parties in the talks, an IRA ceasefire is absolutely necessary. Moreover, a mere reinstatement of the 1994 ceasefire is insufficient ground for Loyalists to accept Sinn Féin in negotiations. What is needed is not an unequivocal restoration of the 1994 ceasefire, but an unequivocal ceasefire, which is an entirely different animal.

For the duration of the 1994 ceasefire, which was declared as total and complete, evident and disturbing military activity was taking place. Loyalists and members of the security forces were targeted and information was gathered about them in preparation for potential assassination. Weapons were progressively developed and tested. Training was still taking place and weaponry was still being procured. This, naturally, did nothing to convince us that the ceasefire had any degree of permanence. While the IRA was on an alleged ceasefire, it was establishing workshops and activating personnel in England in preparation for the subsequent attacks at Canary Wharf and Manchester.

What is required in the event of a new ceasefire is a clear commitment not to initiate another military campaign but effectively to adopt a "no first strike" policy, as Loyalists did in 1995. There must also be a declaration that military activity has ceased. We will not accept an IRA ceasefire as genuine if it continues to target and prepare for a further campaign.

Part Four–1997

The year of 1997 introduced a number of changes into the political dynamics of the Northern Irish peace process. With little room for movement in the negotiations, which were still deadlocked over the issue of decommissioning, hope was placed in the upcoming British general election. On May 1, the sweeping electoral victory of the Labor Party raised expectations of a shift in British government policy as well as a shift in Republican strategy. Progress, however, was delayed by the Northern Ireland council elections on May 21, followed by the onset of the marching season. Thus it was only on July 20 that the IRA called a second ceasefire and provided the opportunity for Sinn Féin to enter the negotiations in September. Sinn Féin's entry into talks prompted the exit of the DUP and UKUP, who now were more convinced than ever that secret concessions had been made and that Northern Ireland was being pushed onto the road to a united Ireland. The UUP, UDP and PUP however continued to participate to ensure that Unionist interests were protected in the negotiations. Changes also occurred with respect to the issues of the negotiations. Decommissioning was moved onto committee level and the talks finally moved toward strand one – relations within Northern Ireland, strand two – relations between Northern Ireland and the Republic, and strand three – relations between Britain and Ireland. While Unionist politicians were still not speaking directly to Republicans by the end of the year, some progress had been made, nevertheless.

■ ■ ■

Republicans Talk Peace, Then Kill
(*Irish Voice* February 9–25, 1997)

On February 12, at 6:30 p.m., an IRA sniper shot dead British soldier Stephen Restorick, who was manning a checkpoint at Bessbrook, County Armagh. The attack was widely perceived as an attempt by the IRA to draw Loyalist para-militaries back into conflict.

The murder of a young British soldier in County Armagh last Wednesday brings into sharp focus the serious implications which continued violence has for an already crumbling peace process. Northern Irish society is becoming filled with despair, and the prospects for a respite in the form of a new IRA cease-fire appear to be non-existent at this time.

Republicans state that they remain committed to their peace strategy, but the product of that strategy was a twenty-three-year-old soldier being shot through the back by an IRA sniper and a civilian being struck in the head by the same bul-let after it left his body. Up until that point, the IRA had launched thirty-eight failed attempts to murder members of the security forces, as well as a Unionist politician, since the new year. This is not activity consistent with the search for a peace-ful settlement.

The question now is what will come next? Naturally, intense speculation surrounds the intentions of Loyalists. The Loyalist ceasefire has remained in place since October 1994 despite intense provocation from the IRA, and Loyalists have continued to play an active role in the multi-party talks process in the hope that some progress can be found toward agreement. Indeed, we will continue to argue that the way forward is through dialogue, not conflict, and will use all influence to pre-vent a Loyalist response to the IRA's violence. Clearly, if the Loyalist ceasefire were to collapse and widespread inter-com-munity conflict were to escalate, then it would be very difficult to foresee how the situation could be salvaged in the short term.

On December 22, 1987 John McMichael was killed by an IRA booby-trap bomb under his car.

John McMichael's funeral. Gary McMichael carrying his father's coffin.

Emergency services and local residents searching for survivors in the wake of the Shankill bomb on October 23, 1993.

Gerry Adams carrying the coffin of the Shankill bomber, Thomas Begley.

Ray Smallwoods

Ray Smallwoods' funeral after he was killed by the IRA on July 11, 1994.

The announcement of the Loyalist ceasefire on October 13, 1994.

(PACEMAKER PRESS INTERNATIONAL)

The UDP after its first meeting with British government officials in
December 1994.

Gary McMichael with US President Bill Clinton in the Oval Office
on March 17, 1998.

Obviously, that scenario is not a welcome one, and is not in anyone's interest. But that is where we are being dragged to, despite the fact that the vast majority of people in Unionist and Nationalist communities do not support further violence. The IRA must appreciate the implications of further violence and recognize the impact upon any prospect of building a peaceful settlement. They must accept that the only way forward is to pursue agreement between our communities through dialogue, and call an immediate and irrevocable ceasefire.

The perceived logic of the Republican campaign is that, by the use and threat of force, they can coerce the British government into making concessions to the IRA on the format and agenda of negotiations. That is, of course, a cynical and dubious logic which ignores the reality of the situation. First of all, Sinn Féin could have joined the negotiation process at the same point as everyone else and under the same conditions. The only obstacle to its participation has been the continued murder campaign of the IRA. It is the party's refusal to bring that campaign to an end that prevents it from taking part in negotiations. That is a wholly reasonable position. Surely, one could not be expected to sit at a table with those who are at the same time trying to kill the others around that table.

The second point relates to the influence that a progression of violence has upon how Republicans are perceived by others. The more IRA violence occurs, the more difficult it is for others to believe that Republicans are committed to democratic values. Gerry Adams has said that he is prepared to sign up to the Mitchell Principles of democracy and non-violence yet, at the same time, he refuses to argue for a new IRA ceasefire. One of the Mitchell Principles requires a commitment to oppose the use or threat of force to influence the course or outcome of negotiations. Strangely, the IRA's tactics at this time are to do exactly that, as they have stated that their violent campaign relates to the format and agenda of the negotiations.

The third and most important point is that peace cannot be arrived at through the use of force adverse to the democratic will of the people. Republicans seek to dictate the manner in which negotiations take place, and to force the British government to alter the current negotiations to favor the Republican movement, without regard to the views of the other participants in those negotiations. Essentially, their so-called peace strategy is based upon the premise that the terms of a settlement must be negotiated directly between Republicans and the British government.

They must learn that it is not the British government with whom peace will be negotiated. It is with the other democratic representatives, who disagree with Sinn Féin's analysis. It is not John Major whom they must convince. It is people like me, because it is not John Major with whom they must learn to share Northern Ireland. They must convince me – and the rest of the population who do not believe in an independent Irish state.

But it seems that they find themselves unable to face the reality of negotiation or compromise. A process of negotiation can only succeed if those around the table, if not trusting one another, can at least feel comfortable with the presence of others. Sinn Féin argues that the process is not inclusive, but inclusiveness is not achieved by Sinn Féin being eased into negotiations under conditions which lead others to leave the room. The actions of Republicans serve no other purpose than to deepen suspicion and distrust within the minds of Unionists and indeed constitutional Nationalists, thereby making the creation of conditions in which negotiations can take place, never mind succeed, increasingly unlikely.

So, Sinn Féin and the IRA will have to decide how they intend to woo everyone else to accept that they are in any way serious about trying to find a democratic settlement, and they will have to recognize the negative role that their current strategy plays in pursuing that objective. Their refusal to argue for a new ceasefire, and their efforts to murder their opponents, do nothing to advance peace. In real terms, it makes Republicanism the biggest single obstacle to peace. Their strategy is entirely counter-productive.

Loyalists have worked against all odds to avoid the conflict, but we are steadily losing grip of what may be the last opportunity for peace. The worst thing about it is that it makes no sense at all. This war does not have to be fought. The IRA must accept that our differences can be addressed through dialogue between the Northern Ireland political parties. They cannot be overcome through force.

It is a pity that some people will still conveniently ignore the IRA's violence. It was sickening for me that, two days after the IRA murdered the young soldier at Bessbrook, a delegation of US congressmen, in a short visit to Northern Ireland, were happy to pose for the press with Gerry Adams and offer him eulogy, while we Loyalists, who are holding the line, were treated by them in an entirely different manner.

Republicans Must Accept Responsibility

(*Irish Voice* March 26–April 1, 1997)

Another St. Patrick's Day reception at the White House . . .

I spent St. Patrick's Day in the White House again this year. The event was a somewhat cosmopolitan affair. Never have I seen such a diverse political representation. Almost all of the Northern Ireland parties were there. I had been at the White House in 1995 when only the UDP, SDLP, Sinn Féin and Alliance Party had accepted the invitation. Now it was awash with the PUP, Ulster Unionists, Northern Ireland Women's Coalition and Northern Ireland Labor Party attending. Even Bob McCartney, leader of the UK Unionist Party, came along, although he should have saved himself the airfare since he didn't speak to anyone there and no one seemed interested in talking to him either.

It is a big step forward that so many were prepared to spend St. Patrick's Day at the White House when it would have been impossible to contemplate this even a few years before. However, I am not sure how some of the Americans coped. For some, it must have been complex enough to grasp the Unionist–Nationalist axis of Northern Ireland politics, only to be confused entirely by exposure to the reality of the political mish-mash which exists. But, for many, the focus was not upon who was there, but upon who was not. IRA violence had excluded Sinn Féin from the invitation list. Yet, despite their absence, conversation evolved around them.

The main issue for political Irish America was clearly the need for an IRA ceasefire. Major speeches had been made by Senator George Mitchell and Senator Edward Kennedy calling for an immediate end to violence. I certainly reinforced the view that a new ceasefire is central to the continuation of the peace process. The peace process has been seriously damaged by the re-emergence of violence. The only thing which has kept the process alive at all has been the refusal of Loyalists to be drawn back into full-scale conflict. But time is steadily running out. The strains imposed by the IRA activity are becoming more evident and the overall environment is deteriorating rapidly.

I had seriously questioned whether it was prudent to travel to the US at all while there is so much to attend to on our own doorstep. Around the time of our visit, there were attacks on the police, causing serious injuries, a Republican was killed in Belfast, a series of rural Orange halls were destroyed by arsonists. All are actions which confirm that the situation is getting out of control. There is only one cure which will prevent my country becoming engulfed in full-scale conflict: an IRA ceasefire. If a ceasefire does not come, then I believe that wider confrontation is inescapable.

The window of opportunity is there for all to see. The forthcoming United Kingdom general election provides the perfect chance for Republicans to bring their violence to a halt. The political landscape could be significantly altered at this time and the process could become revitalized when all-party talks resume on June 3. The question is, will the IRA take the opportunity presented to it?

There is a clear consensus that it is the only logical choice. But it is difficult to see logic in the IRA's present strategy. However, most anticipate that a ceasefire will come before or shortly after the general election. There are many theories. For some unknown reason, David Trimble was telling everyone at the White House that there would be a ceasefire on April 10. So, I conclude, this is the only day for sure that there won't be.

I think it is likely that there will be a ceasefire, probably shortly after the election. Of course, the environment could be significantly affected by what may happen between now and then. It is equally likely that the IRA will attempt to leave their current campaign in a spectacular fashion. The conditions which surround a new ceasefire will determine what attitude Unionists take toward Republicans. The singular Republican focus has been to ensure an immediate invitation to take part in the talks, subsequent to a ceasefire, making the talks "inclusive," as they would term it. I want to see an inclusive process and I believe that a new government will issue an invitation to Sinn Féin in the event of a ceasefire of any description. Inclusiveness, however, is not a concept solely related to Sinn Féin. Inclusiveness is not advanced if, by Sinn Féin's inclusion, other participants withdraw.

Republicans would argue that it is not their problem. But it is their problem; it's a problem for all of us. The success or failure of the peace process is a collective responsibility. There is deep and understandable suspicion of the IRA, following the collapse of its ceasefire and the trauma inflicted upon our society as a result. One cannot pretend that the events since Canary Wharf simply did not happen or that they were justifiable and, therefore, should be written off.

Regardless of the rationale which surrounded the IRA decision to return to violence, the ceasefire failed and as a result the climate has changed. Republicans claim that they need assurances in advance of another ceasefire but we need assurances also, that there is an absolute commitment to ending the violence for good. I find it deeply uncomfortable that Republicans demand that everyone must address the anxieties and concerns they feel to encourage them to take steps toward another ceasefire, but they choose to ignore the fears and uncertainties felt by my community. This is not a formula that will make the search for peace an easy one.

If Republicans truly want inclusive negotiations, then they must accept the responsibility to make it possible for Unionists to justify remaining within the process. If the ceasefire is a restatement of the 1994 cessation, under the same terms, then I believe it will be impossible for any Unionist party to accept Sinn Féin's inclusion, including mine. It must be understood that the 1994 ceasefire brought with it all of the activity related to terrorist action, except the actual execution of the operations. Loyalists were still being targeted for future assassination. IRA personnel were being trained and new weapons were being made for operations such as the bombing of Canary Wharf.

Loyalists were aware of some of these activities at the time, but they reluctantly gave Republicans the benefit of the doubt. That will not be the case again. Republicans must take steps to build confidence within the Unionist community and enable the process to move forward in a revitalized environment in which meaningful negotiation can take place.

Don't Expect Any Sudden Changes

(*Irish Voice* April 30–May 6, 1997)

With the British general elections scheduled for May 1, the majority of people of Northern Ireland hoped that a change in government would revitalize the peace process.

Thursday, May 1 is the British general election. The people of Britain are widely anticipating a change in government, with the first Labor administration in eighteen years. I think there is very little chance that the Conservatives will be able to recover the lost ground at this late stage, and perhaps it is a time when the entire country simply wants a change of power. What a Labor government will bring for Britain is difficult to foretell, but most people believe that it can't be any worse than what eighteen years of Tory rule has brought.

Many in Northern Ireland are also waiting with anticipation for the outcome of the elections, though for quite different motives than those in Great Britain. The Labor Party is not organized in Northern Ireland and denies its residents membership; therefore we have no say in who takes power. Policy toward Northern Ireland from the Tories, Labor and Liberal Democrats has also been virtually identical and, as such, there is very little to look forward to. We will experience the benefits or otherwise of this election in due course as decisions are foisted upon us by an unaccountable, if new, government.

Some think that a Labor administration will bring impetus to the peace process and that it may revitalize the talks process when it is reconvened on June 3. Indeed, the IRA and Sinn Féin are counting on it. They say that there will not be any ceasefire while there is a Tory government in place. But I think that it would be unwise to think that any new government, particularly a brand that has been out of power for almost two decades, will be rushing to make any great changes in the short term until they have a strong feel for the reins. This is particularly so in Northern Ireland.

It is expected that Mo Mowlam will become the new Secretary of State but, despite her intimacy with Northern Ireland and her straight-talking dynamic manner, I can't see her taking any serious risks with the peace process upon her arrival. And, judging from the attitude some would take toward her, it may take some time to get settled in.

I think changes in support among Northern Ireland parties may have a greater impact upon the peace process and where it will go from here. Sinn Féin is pinning its hopes upon gaining two or three Westminster seats and is playing it for all it is worth, putting the emphasis on the need for such a success to strengthen its hand for another ceasefire. That tactic worked in the 1996 forum elections, raising Sinn Féin's vote up to 15%, but it remains to be seen whether it will work this time around.

People thought last year that the elevated vote would be used as a lever for a ceasefire, but a few days later the IRA blew the heart out of Manchester and widened its terrorist campaign, leaving a lot of people feeling conned. It would also be a significant kick in the teeth for SDLP leader John Hume, who is expected to lose one of his party's seats to Sinn Féin. It will signal a shift of support toward the extreme and away from the constitutional non-violent Nationalism which he represents. He has gone as far as describing a vote for Sinn Féin as a vote for the IRA's campaign of murder.

There could be changes within Unionism also. There is a very real chance that, partly due to boundary changes, the Reverend William McCrea of the DUP could lose his seat to Sinn Féin, and that the DUP deputy leader Peter Robinson could run foul of a challenge by the Ulster Unionist Party. If such a scenario were to unfold, Ian Paisley would find himself being his party's only sitting Member of Parliament. If Peter Robinson were to lose his seat, it would be interpreted as a rejection of the very negative attitude of the DUP in the multi-party talks.

Whatever changes may take place will certainly impact to some degree upon the course of negotiations when they resume, but by no means is it certain that any change in emphasis will be enough to help the talks progress significantly. Sadly, the major factor remains whether the IRA will remove their campaign of violence. While such terrorism continues, the presence of Sinn Féin at the talks cannot even be considered, and the talks are unlikely to succeed in an atmosphere polluted by violence.

Unfortunately, at this moment, it seems that Republicans are not interested in calling a ceasefire before the resumption of talks. They are indicating that there will be no question of one unless their conditions are met yet, at the same time, they are somewhat paradoxically arguing that no preconditions can be placed upon them. The fact is the only precondition is that those who sit around the table do so in the same circumstances as everybody else. That precludes the use or threat of violence. It is surely not unreasonable for us to ask that those who expect us to negotiate with them respect the same terms as all others. That means a new ceasefire. That is one thing that cannot be bargained with.

Unionists Are Desperate for Change
(*Irish Voice* June 4-10, 1997)

On May 21, local government elections were held in Northern Ireland. The voter turnout among Unionists was low, reflecting apathy and election fatigue. The result was a Nationalist gain in Belfast and west of the Bann, dealing a psychological blow to Unionism.

Local government elections recently concluded in Northern Ireland, the results causing a great deal of debate. The political landscape has changed somewhat, largely because of the different approaches that the Unionist and Nationalist electorates took to the election. The Nationalist vote was up and there was a rise in the support for Sinn Féin. John Hume's SDLP has lost quite a number of seats to Republicans, and Sinn Féin now has an equal number of seats to those of the Ulster Unionist Party in Belfast City Council.

Also, voting patterns dramatically changed in the Unionist community, or should I say non-voting patterns. The turnout in Unionist areas generally was extremely poor, with only 30–40% voting in some. There has been a lot of speculation about the reason for this, but it is widely attributed to voter apathy. I believe that many people throughout the Unionist community feel depressed about the peace process as a whole, and specifically find it difficult to identify with the approach that traditional Unionist parties are taking to it. The concern felt toward the political intentions of the British and Irish governments, coupled with the increased threat to society posed by IRA terrorism, would have historically provided a stampede to the polling stations and an inflation of the extreme Democratic Unionist Party (DUP) vote.

The opposite has occurred in this instance. I think we have reached a watershed within Unionism. The electorate has come to a point where it fails to see what the Ulster Unionist Party (UUP) or the DUP have to offer. For twenty-five years they have witnessed the steady demise of Unionism through political incompetence, and are now beginning to experience what they never thought possible – extreme Republicanism gaining prominence over constitutional Nationalism. The UUP and DUP have singularly failed to provide any form of political leadership and have stagnated. Over the past year, the Unionist parties have only succeeded in ensuring the gridlock of the talks process, while Sinn Féin has the talks process on a short leash.

Rather than those who have chosen to follow the democratic path moving forward and beyond those who fail to embrace the democratic process, and therefore setting the challenge to Republicans, the predictability of Unionists over the decommissioning issue has led to the entire process becoming dependent on the actions of Republicans. The Unionist electorate is fed up with incompetence and is looking for a more innovative approach. That is demonstrated by the fact that, while the traditional Unionist vote declined, the support for the Loyalist parties soared. The Ulster Democratic Party (UDP) and the Progressive Unionist Party (PUP) now for the first time have a significant representation on Belfast City Council, and in other areas have doubled the existing vote. This is a signal that people want to embrace a variety of Unionism which is imaginative, intelligent and pro-active.

I can only hope that the UUP and the DUP recognize the message that the voters were sending them for what it is. The Unionist people are saying that it's time for them to get their act together. Whether that will translate into a new approach in the talks process when it resumes on June 3 remains to be seen. The shift in Nationalist voting patterns is something which one must consider also. It seems apparent that more and more people are turning toward Sinn Féin, and that these people seem more relaxed about the relationship between Sinn Féin and Republican violence. Some would interpret that as evidence that the wider Nationalist community is supportive of the IRA's campaign, but I think that is an erroneous assumption.

Sinn Féin is increasing its support for a number of reasons. Firstly, the difficulty which many may have had with the IRA's violence has been made more palatable by the fact that the IRA has temporarily suspended its campaign until the elections in the south are out of the way, and indeed to facilitate contact between it and the British government. Secondly, Sinn Féin has worked very hard to blur the line between Nationalism and Republicanism by exploiting the relationship between John Hume and Gerry Adams to its full potential, thereby elevating Sinn Féin to a level of acceptability similar to that of the SDLP. Thirdly, Sinn Féin has been pro-active in its pursuit of Nationalist–Republican objectives, always keeping pressure on "the Brits." That assertiveness, particularly in an environment at present absent of violence, is an attractive feature to the wider Nationalist community.

Most importantly, however, once again many people are hoping that increased support for Sinn Féin will strengthen the chances of a new ceasefire. I do not subscribe to the view of some that this is a permanent transfer of support away from the SDLP. Listening to people, I believe that this is a temporary lending of support to advance the peace process. Sinn Féin must recognize this for what it is. If it does not deliver the ceasefire, particularly at a time when there is no obvious reason for delay, then that support will inevitably recede. Unfortunately, what we have experienced in recent times is that an increase in Sinn Féin's mandate has been interpreted as an endorsement of the IRA strategy and results in Republicans upping the ante even further.

Loyalists Won't Hand Over Arms

(*Irish Voice* July 2–8, 1997)

On July 1, Northern Ireland Secretary Mo Mowlam and Irish Taoiseach Bertie Ahern met to discuss the British–Irish compromise proposals on decommissioning.

The peace process has reached a defining point. Tough decisions will have to be made in the coming weeks by the participants in the multi-party talks, and by those who remain outside that process. The announcement by Tony Blair of proposals to address the decommissioning issue, and his indication of a time frame for the commencement of substantive negotiations holds potential for pushing the entire process into a new stage.

The initiative is recognition that, having found it impossible to resolve the difficult matter of decommissioning during many months of discussion, a determination of that debate must occur to allow substantive negotiations to begin. For, if we do not move forward quickly, there will be little opportunity to pursue a comprehensive agreement, as the talks will come to an end in May 1998.

The arms issue is a matter which should not have had the prominence it has in the peace process. Yet it is an issue which must, nevertheless, be addressed. We look forward to agreement being reached upon how that will be achieved, but such agreement must reflect the realities involved. It has been proposed that a commission should be created to pursue the decommissioning of illegal arms and that it should relate to the talks process by way of a sub-committee which will liaise between the two. Additionally, another committee will address confidence-building issues such as prisoners, policing, etc.

What is of obvious concern is that the progress of the negotiations will become relative to the progress being made by the commission. That would, of course, be unacceptable. Arms cannot be used as a bargaining chip for political progress. Neither will we accept attempts to barter prisoner release for arms. Moreover, it would be unwise to suppose that the creation of a commission will in itself deliver a speedy removal of arms from our society. First of all, one must not underestimate the practical difficulties which may arise, even assuming that the will exists on all sides to make it a reality.

But, more importantly, those who argue for the removal of weapons must dispel any notion they may have that any such process will be complied with by Loyalists while Republicans remain on the outside and engaged in a violent campaign. Loyalists will not become crash test dummies for decommissioning or jump through hoops for anyone. Indeed, it is inconceivable that Loyalists would become complicit in a process which would leave their community defenseless against continued Republican aggression, or until the potential for such aggression has been removed.

This brings me to the other major decision which must be made in the very near future. It is make up your mind time for Republicans. They must now decide whether they are prepared to enter the political process or if they are going to continue their armed aggression. Their strategy of Tactical Use of Armed Struggle (TUAS) is not tenable. If they are not prepared to call a ceasefire now, then the talks process must forge ahead immediately, leaving behind those who do not wish to join the democratic process. The IRA has been given every possible opportunity to come back into the process but has refused to do so at every turn. The supposed desire on the part of Republicans to engage in meaningful negotiations is starkly at odds with the brutal reality pointed up by recent events.

The British government took a risky step by re-opening contact with Sinn Féin and allowing two meetings to take place, during which, it has now been revealed, Tony Blair's government presented Republicans with terms for an entry to negotiations. The IRA knew that another meeting had been arranged to take those discussions further. Yet, it callously murdered two community policemen in Lurgan by walking up behind them and shooting them in the backs of their heads. The government subsequently cut off contact with Republicans in response to this atrocity.

No logic can be attached to the IRA's action except that it may have deliberately scuppered the opportunity of further government contact. Why would Republicans do this? It is not because their movement is split, as some would argue, or that there was a communications breakdown. The IRA is united and the relationship between it and Sinn Féin is intrinsic to the dual strategy.

There is no justifiable reason why Republicans should not bring about another ceasefire unless they really do not want to be part of the present process. It is becoming increasingly evident that the only rationale which can be attached to the Republican position is that it refuses to accept a place in the peace process because it cannot come to terms with the implications of negotiations. I hope that I will be proved wrong, but it seems unlikely that the IRA/Sinn Féin stand will take this last opportunity to be part of a democratic settlement. Unfortunately, the result of that failure is likely to be an escalation of Republican violence with an aim to force the negotiations to collapse and to provoke a Loyalist response to their aggression.

It is vital that there is no tolerance from any quarter for those who are prepared not only to squander their own opportunity to be part of a new peace settlement, but also to destroy that opportunity for everyone else in Northern Ireland. Republicans must recognize that there is no future in continued aggression, and that the only way forward is to call an immediate and irrevocable ceasefire and to assist in the creation of an environment which will make a political settlement possible.

Republicans' Turn to Move

(*Irish Voice* July 16–22, 1997)

On July 12 every year, Orangemen celebrate the victory of King William at the Battle of the Boyne. According to the Orange Order, the Boyne is celebrated not because the victory guaranteed the Protestant Ascendancy but because it set in motion the shift from absolutism to parliamentary democracy, guaranteeing civil and religious liberties for all.

The "Twelfth" is a time when Protestants celebrate the historical victory of King William of Orange over the Catholic King James at the Battle of the Boyne in 1690. It is the pinnacle of the Protestant cultural calendar, with tens of thousands of people taking part in or watching the proceedings which take place in a carnival-type atmosphere. The event itself is perhaps now more important and relevant than the moment in Irish history which it commemorates. I remember as a child relishing the festivities which surrounded the "Twelfth," street parties on the eleventh night and the trek to the "Twelfth" field the next day. It was a joyful time.

But now it represents a time of great anguish and anxiety. Many people dread the approach of the "Twelfth" for it has become synonymous with conflict and confrontation. The past three years have made sure of that. Where before, most people had never even heard of Drumcree, it is now seared into the minds of every single person in this land. It has become the symbolic capital of the ongoing struggle between the two traditions in Northern Ireland.

Orange parades seemed not to be a tremendously important issue until three years ago. The parades, which have now been deemed contentious, have been taking place for some two hundred years in some cases, without much reason for attention. Now each occasion is a pitched battle. The residents' group which Republicans created initially in the Lower Ormeau Road area of Belfast has been cloned in a dozen other areas which have now become central to the parades controversy, not least Drumcree. There are new residents' protest groups being manufactured in Belfast, particularly in the East and North of the city, in advance of next year's marching season. The objective is to cause as much disruption and chaos as possible, specifically in interface areas.

The people of Northern Ireland have been spiraling down into despair, recognizing the potential of the parades problem to bring our society literally to the point of civil war. The decision at Drumcree this year evidenced that potential. The level of violence was astounding, the provocation intense. IRA and INLA gunmen used the street violence as a cover to launch an offensive against the police and the Protestant community right across the province. A fourteen-year-old boy was wounded when a Republican fired across the peace-line, Protestant businesses in Catholic areas and Orange halls were burned to the ground, and Protestant families were attacked and forced from their homes.

The question of the rights and wrongs of the Drumcree decision is irrelevant. The parade decisions made by the RUC reflect the dilemma of gauging the potential level of threat of violence from one side against the threat of violence from the other. There are no rights or wrongs involved in that decision-making process. It is simply a least-worst-case formula.

Society has been brought almost to its knees in the past week and I am convinced that, if the level of confrontation and violence which was being planned by Republicans at parade flashpoints and the subsequent Loyalist responses to that had taken place, then the situation would have become irretrievable. It is against that backdrop that I can say that I now believe that the decision taken by the Orange Order to cancel or re-route its most contentious parades on the "Twelfth" has averted disaster.

Sinn Féin Needs to Learn Honesty
(*Irish Voice* October 1–7, 1997)

On September 9, Sinn Féin entered the negotiations and accepted the Mitchell Principles. Sinn Féin's position, however, was questioned when the IRA released a statement that it had "a problem with sections of the Mitchell Principles."

The all-party talks in Belfast have taken a momentous step forward. The decommissioning issue, which has occupied the discussions for much of the time, has finally been overcome, and the way is clear for negotiations on the substantive issues to take place. The Ulster Democratic Party has been waiting for this moment since we joined the talks in June of last year. Now that it has arrived, the enormity of the challenge facing us is all too stark to see. The prospect of agreement is severely hampered by the short time-frame, the negotiations having a life span that ends in May of next year.

The participants should ask themselves what disservice they have done to the people of Northern Ireland by their selfish approaches, which have frittered away the last fifteen months. The Unionist obsession with decommisioning, and the Republican refusal to end its terrorism and enter negotiations, have been serious impediments. But rapid progress has now been made, following the courageous decision by Ulster Unionist Party leader David Trimble to remain in the talks alongside the UDP and the Progressive Unionist Party despite the exit of Ian Paisley's Democratic Unionist Party. The outstanding issues have been overcome and the substantive negotiations are scheduled to be launched shortly.

The success of the negotiations will depend upon the will of the participants to reach an accommodative settlement. But agreement among the parties alone is not enough. Ultimately, it will be the people of Northern Ireland as a whole who will decide the outcome. If whatever emerges from the talks is rejected by the people of Northern Ireland at the subsequent referendum, then it cannot be implemented. That is the consent principle which forms the basis of the process in which we are engaged.

The parameters of a future settlement are dictated by realms of what is realistically achievable. Therefore, the onus is on the parties to work toward a settlement that will not only appeal to their own specific constituency, but which can command widespread support across the community. That is a daunting challenge indeed in our divided society. It will only be achievable if those who negotiate can do so in an environment of trust and confidence. A severe difficulty I see at present is that the potential for such trust is not plainly evident. I have a responsibility to convince others of our commitment and that our position should be accepted in good faith.

That will be difficult, but Loyalists will attempt to do so. Equally, Republicans must find ways to convince others that they genuinely seek an accommodative settlement. The evidence thus far has done little to suggest a desire to do so. How can one negotiate in good faith or accept Sinn Féin's position in good faith when it refuses even to be up front and honest with the rest of us in this process about who it is, and who it represents?

Sinn Féin has gone some way over the past two weeks to tell us that it has no relationship with the IRA, that whatever comes out of the talks has no impact on the position of the IRA. In a recent issue of *An Phoblacht*, the IRA moved away from the Mitchell Principles of democracy and non-violence which participants must commit themselves to uphold in order to take a place at the talks. Sinn Féin had signed up to the Mitchell Principles two days before.

There is a deliberate and very dishonest tactic being employed. Republicans are trying to create a gap between Sinn Féin and the IRA so that they can involve themselves in the negotiation process but, at the same time, hold the option of reverting to military action if required. The IRA is seeking to create an environment where Sinn Féin will not be culpable whatsoever in the eventuality of the IRA reverting to violence.

That is obviously an untenable position. Firstly, there is little scope for an accommodative settlement if Republicans are preparing for a situation in which Sinn Féin can maintain its position at the negotiating table while the IRA is murdering the others around that table. Secondly, Republicans are, by divorcing the two sides of the Republican coin, distancing themselves from having to accept any outcome of the negotiations. Even if the talks are a success, the IRA is reserving the right to oppose the outcome through terror.

When Sinn Féin talks to the IRA, it talks to itself. They are the same organization, yet they are attempting to create the illusion that they are not. I wonder if those in Ireland or America who have expended so much of their time and energy to get Sinn Féin to the negotiating table doubted for one minute that they were, in fact, bringing the IRA to the table? I wonder how they feel now, when Sinn Féin at that very table is saying, "Sorry, lads, we don't speak for the Provos. Whatever gave you that idea?" Who do they think they are trying to kid? Sinn Féin does have a substantial political mandate, but its relevance to the peace process stretches far beyond that mandate. The strategy is transparent and no one is being fooled by it. But it is a dangerous path to go down. If they do not catch themselves on and face up to their responsibilities, they risk destroying the peace process entirely.

Loyalists have remained committed to the objective of bringing peace to the people of Northern Ireland through a democratic settlement. We will not walk away from our responsibilities, but neither will we be taken for a ride by Republicans. There will be no direct dialogue between Loyalists and Sinn Féin as long as such behavior continues. There is no point in negotiating with people who cannot even be honest about their own position in the talks. We will negotiate with those other parties who have honestly committed themselves to this process and who are genuinely endeavoring to find a purely democratic solution to this conflict.

Compromise Is the Key to Success
(*Irish Voice* October 29-November 4, 1997)

With the issue of decommissioning moved to committee level, negotiations tentatively moved on to substantive issues.

When the IRA finally put a halt to its terrorist campaign, we had reached a point where the environment was so contaminated that it seemed unlikely that wider conflict could be avoided. That was an important step. The subsequent decision by the Ulster Unionists not to walk away from the process following Sinn Féin's inclusion was another.

Together they marked a turning point in Northern Ireland's troubled history. For three years, Loyalists have been waiting for the day when serious negotiations would take place and the people would be given their first real opportunity to find a peaceful and democratic resolution of this conflict. That is where we are today.

The process of negotiations has been under way for a few weeks now. The participants are taking their first tentative steps toward meeting the greatest challenge they have ever faced. But the true enormity of the task has perhaps not as yet sunk in.

We have a time-frame to meet which gives us just seven months to overcome hundreds of years of division. It may be possible; it may not. Success will depend on our capacity to use the time available wisely. Essentially, what is required is for all participants to move beyond ideological rhetoric, which has dogged our society over the course of this conflict, to a new level of debate. We must possess the strength to leave behind romantic ideals and concentrate upon creating a new society which can cater for the needs of all our people.

There are parameters that guide these negotiations. While each party can be expected to seek to negotiate the best terms for its constituency, if every party holds to its manifesto position there is no chance of agreement. This especially holds true for

Sinn Féin. That party approaches the negotiations in pursuit of an independent unitary state which, while it may be an entirely legitimate aspiration in the context of these negotiations, is not a realizable one. If we are realistically to reach agreement we must all begin the search at least within the same ball-park. Sinn Féin will not succeed in convincing everyone else that the best way forward is a united Ireland. Nor will Unionists convince everyone else of the merits of full integration with the rest of the UK. The reality of the situation which must be grasped is that, whatever the nature and form of relationships, the outcome will reflect Northern Ireland's continuing membership of the United Kingdom.

But, within that context, we can pursue agreement on new structures in Northern Ireland that can command widespread cross-community support, that celebrate our diversity and offer equality and respect for all. Competing claims to Northern Ireland have only served to deepen divisions, by forcing people to choose on questions of identity and allegiance. Competing claims have forced the extremes of both traditions on to the center stage of politics. As the past thirty years have shown, a society run from the extremes ends up at war with itself.

The focus of these negotiations should be to devise structures which address Northern Ireland's sense of uniqueness and which can command the support and allegiance of both main traditions. Common ground exists, but it must be given a chance. Removing any constitutional uncertainties on the status of Northern Ireland must be the beginning. Indeed, the continuing boundary dispute has become an anachronism when borders are disappearing all over Europe, and when the economies of Europe and the United States are striving toward cooperation in an age of globalization.

We seek to create democratic structures and a society in which each person is treated equally and with respect. A framework which would allow those who seek constitutional change to pursue their aspirations in a peaceful and democratic fashion – where all change is possible if it commands sufficient cross-community support. The driving force of the negotiations must not be what is aspired to, but what is possible in the context of this process. Clearly, the outcome will not be to the complete satisfaction of all, but can be one within which each of us can coexist in the absence of conflict. At the end of the day, if the talks become no more than a battle of wits, they will not succeed. For there to be any level of success, each of the main traditions must guarantee one another's future in any new structures.

There can be no successful outcome unless both Unionists and Nationalists agree. Therefore, it is in both our interests to work toward an arrangement within which each of us can live comfortably. There is the additional question of sustainability. We have a responsibility not only to ensure that the process can encourage support across both traditions but that the level of such support is significant enough to ensure that a settlement can be successfully applied and sustained for the foreseeable future. We are not interested in a short-term or interim arrangement, but are in pursuit of a durable and lasting settlement.

My Dad's Death Won't Be in Vain
(*Irish Voice* December 17–30, 1997)

On December 22, 1987, John McMichael was killed by an IRA booby-trap bomb planted under his car at his home in Lisburn.

Christmas time for most people is a joyful time. A time for celebration and fellowship. An occasion when families find their troubles eclipsed by goodwill and togetherness. It is a period that people look forward to. I used to, but no more. I dread the coming of Christmas. For, to me, it is a time of sorrow. I lost my father at Christmas. He was murdered.

This year is particularly difficult for it is the tenth anniversary of his death. I have found myself reflecting over the time that has passed and the things that have happened since that turning point in my life. For it was indeed a turning point. I was eighteen when he died, on the threshold of adulthood, and as is normal at that age, I was facing many choices, searching for direction. When my father was killed, it shattered my life. That event more than any other has fundamentally influenced the choices I have had to make in life. The loss of a parent is a traumatic occurrence at any time, but more so when it is violent or unexpected.

My father was murdered when the IRA put a booby-trap bomb under his car, three days before Christmas in 1987. He was thirty-nine years old. He was a well-known political figure and, consequently, we knew he was in harm's way. But while the danger of assassination was an ever-present worry, knowing it is possible does not prepare you for the trauma of sudden, violent death. There had been numerous previous attempts on his life, and I was aware of that, but I did not expect that my father would die so young.

We go through our lives understanding the reality of being captured in a society at war with itself, but only those who have experienced its effects directly can appreciate the true horror of conflict. Three-and-a-half thousand families have undergone the same experience I have. I often wonder how such tragedy has affected the people in each of those families, and how it has altered their lives.

When I look back, I wonder where would I be now if my father had not died? I know that I would not be doing what I am now. It is because of his death that I became involved in politics. The emotions that ran through me at that time could have sent me in any direction. I had to fight the bitterness I felt toward those who had taken him from me, to resist the temptation to succumb to my emotion and become embroiled in the conflict myself. Many more have lost that fight and, subsequently, their own lives or freedom.

Yet, I could not stand by and allow my country to implode either. My father, in the final period of his life, had been struggling vigorously to inject a positive dynamic to the search for an end to conflict. Those who saw an end to conflict as a threat killed him, and I was not prepared to allow those people to prevail.

The UDP has been working since then with a determination to remove the specter of conflict and to oppose those who have sought to force their political will upon my community by violent aggression. In 1991, we successfully persuaded the Loyalist paramilitary groupings to end their military campaign to facilitate political talks under the then Northern Ireland Secretary of State, Peter Brooke. This was a signal that there was real potential to transcend the physical conflict. The IRA refused to reciprocate and opposed the talks process, escalating sectarian attacks and soon after, murdered two of our members in Londonderry. Our peace effort was unsuccessful. However, we remained undeterred and committed to creating hope in what seemed a hopeless situation.

The Northern Ireland peace process has been through many stages, and this was just one of them. The IRA was not ready for the challenge then and is now still grappling to make the transition from physical force to the currency of non-violent democratic politics. It remains to be seen if the current stage of the process will reach fruition, and whether we shall go further toward removing the division which plagues our society. The odds are stacked against us, our communities are racked with doubt, and the intolerance that prevents rapprochement remains. Yet there is still a real potential to move forward.

Recently, people who are opposed to the peace process killed a man in North Belfast. The man was a Catholic and was the chairman of a GAA club. That is neither here nor there. He need not have died. I grieve with his family, for I know their hurt, and his death is another unnecessary casualty of the conflict. There will probably be more such deaths until our society learns to come to terms with itself. The challenge to us all is to transcend the intolerance which leads to people carrying out such acts, and to change fundamentally attitudes toward the value of human life. Society is changing, but not quickly enough. That process is hampered by an inability to overcome our prejudices and a reluctance to be seen to desecrate the memory of our respective dead.

When I look over the past decade and undergo the torture of self-analysis, I constantly wonder whether my father would have approved of the actions, risks and decisions I have taken. Part of me has had to suppress my hurt in order to make some of the choices I have made. Making peace does not mean that one has to forgive those who have inflicted pain upon us, or forget the costs incurred in this conflict. I, for one, will never forgive those who took a piece of my life away. But each of us has a responsibility to honor their memory by preventing others undergoing the same pain.

A commission has been set up to investigate ways to remember the victims of the conflict. Should there be a memorial erected to commemorate them? What would it say and where should we put it? Several tons of granite, wherever it is placed, will not adequately do those people justice. The only fitting memorial is a positive outcome of the talks and the creation of a new society in which not one further single person will lose his or her life through violence, and in which no other family will go through the anguish and suffering that I and so many others have endured.

Part Five–1998

The year of 1998, despite its ominous beginning, will go down in history as the year a negotiated settlement truly ended the conflict in Northern Ireland. The INLA murder of Billy Wright in the Maze Prison on December 27, 1997, followed by the murder of Loyalist Jim Guiney led to UFF retaliation. On January 26, the UDP was excluded from negotiations as a result. The IRA broke its ceasefire, murdering Loyalist Robert Dougan, leading to Sinn Féin's expulsion from the talks in February. In March, with everyone back around the negotiating table, substantial negotiations on strands one, two and three finally began. The result was the Good Friday Agreement on April 10. The Agreement was put to the people of Northern Ireland and the Republic on May 22 and was overwhelmingly supported. Elections for the Northern Ireland Assembly followed on June 25, putting in place new structures of governance. The first real test for the Agreement came with the Drumcree Orange parade in July. Despite the prolonged stand-off and violence, the decision of the Parades Commission not to allow the march down the Garvaghy Road was upheld; the Agreement and peace survived.

■ ■ ■

Peace Is Still Possible
(*Ireland on Sunday* January 4, 1998)

On December 27, 1997, Loyalist Volunteer Force leader Billy Wright was shot dead in the Maze Prison by members of the INLA. His murder triggered a spate of Loyalist reprisal killings.

It would appear that the peace process is running into the ground. The worsening security situation coupled with the increasing demoralization throughout the community offers little optimism for the future. It is now time to take stock of the situation and evaluate how we can instill faith in the peace process.

The recent spate of violence has clearly been orchestrated to cause maximum damage to the process and has the potential to pull our entire society back into the depths of conflict once again. The LVF and the INLA exist in opposition to the efforts of those trying to bring peace to Northern Ireland. They have worked to undermine those efforts for the duration of this peace process and, unfortunately, they seem to be succeeding. Violence begets violence and history tells us that a run of killings such as we have seen recently will soon become self-sustaining and others will be drawn into the fray. That is the brutal reality of where we are right now. The murder of Billy Wright was a spark designed to ignite a fire.

This must be considered against a background of dissatisfaction with the direction of the overall process and the snail's pace of the negotiations. The Unionist community no longer feels a sense of common ownership of the process. What we have is a society which is demoralized and, therefore, no longer resilient against a return to war.

The negotiations are due to reconvene on January 12, but already there are threats from the PUP that they will not be there. I think this is a serious misjudgment on their part. Their stance assists the enemies of peace and adds further despair to an already vulnerable community. The difficulties that have emerged must be remedied from within the process, not from the outside. The UDP intends to be at the talks table to deal with the problems that exist – and there are many.

In any peace process designed to overcome division and conflict, common ownership is key to its viability. For the negotiations to succeed, there must be a comfortable environment in which the parties can work. Otherwise, the trust and confidence which are necessary on all sides for fruitful negotiation to take place, will not be cultivated. What we have experienced over an extended period is the gradual but steady alienation of the Unionist tradition. It is perceived that the fruits of this process are designed to fall solely at the feet of Nationalism. A lopsided approach to confidence-building areas is the key indicator to this, where it is seen that matters of concern to Nationalists are being addressed, while no reciprocal measures are taken to build confidence among Unionists.

We have seen a policing review take place and the presentation of a Police Bill to Westminster. Legislation empowers a Parades Commission to enforce decisions against Orange parades but not to impose its decision upon protesters. There is movement on IRA prisoners from Britain to the Republic in a funnelling process that will lead to early release – yet there are no measures which affect Loyalist prisoners. Together, all these measures are seen as evidence that the approach to this process by the British government is of a purely partisan nature.

We created a confidence-building committee as part of the negotiations, but it does not negotiate any of these issues, since both the British and Irish governments are fulfilling that agenda independently of the talks. There is a growing belief that we are witnessing the implementation of agreements already reached between the governments and the IRA as part of the facilitation of a renewed ceasefire. If this is the case, then both governments have already destroyed this process. Unless the imbalance is redressed and faith restored, I fear it will all unravel.

Loyalists have kept this process alive over the past three years. When the IRA revoked its 1994 ceasefire, Loyalists did not allow the process to be killed off. The Loyalist commitment to the resolution of the conflict is unquestioned, but it is clear that the government values the IRA ceasefire and Nationalist concerns more highly than those of Loyalists. Despite the Loyalist ceasefire having been in place for almost three-and-a-half years, there has been no recognition of Loyalist commitment from the government. Loyalist prisoners watch IRA inmates being released early while they remain incarcerated.

I want to see the peace process succeed. The UDP is fundamentally committed to reaching a political solution, but the conditions must be correct to facilitate that. When the talks reconvene, there will be ten working weeks available to conclude the negotiations. As long as there is no confidence in the process within a major section of society, it is difficult to envisage such a feat. The British government and that of the Irish Republic must face their responsibilities at this time and recognize that this process is crumbling. The lopsided approach to it must be redressed and confidence rebuilt where it has been eroded. The peace process must be shoved back onto the rails so that we may bring a fair and equitable peace to our society and foil the efforts of the LVF, INLA and others like them.

British Government Needs to Address the Prisoner Issue

(*Ireland on Sunday* January 11, 1998)

Continuing violence placed enormous strain on the peace process and made the early release of prisoners a particularly sensitive subject. In an attempt to salvage the situation, Secretary of State Marjorie Mowlam made an unprecedented visit to the Maze Prison.

A week is a long time in politics. That's what they say. Well, the past week has been a particularly long and eventful one, and the peace process is facing one of its most serious challenges to date. The decision by the UDA/UFF political prisoners last Sunday to withdraw support for the UDP's continued participation in the negotiations was a body blow that took the process to the edge of destruction. No one should be surprised by the strength of feeling among the prisoners. The failure to make progress at the talks before Christmas, combined with the series of concessions engaged over the past few months designed to build Republican confidence, seriously eroded confidence throughout the Unionist community. It also led the prisoners to conclude that this process was incapable of producing a fair and equitable outcome.

My colleagues and I took immediate steps to speak directly to the UDA/UFF prisoners in an effort to convince them to reassess their position. Unfortunately, our arguments did not produce the desired result and a frantic series of meetings were embarked upon in Belfast and London with the objective of ensuring that the government would accept its responsibility to address the crisis. I feel that the subsequent decision by Mo Mowlam to visit the Maze prison to hear the prisoners' views for herself was a courageous and helpful step. Those who criticized her initiative and the earlier visit by David Trimble, should consider for themselves what risks they would take if it would aid the peace process.

We have been accused of brinkmanship by some and by Gerry Adams of playing the "Orange card," but I can assure you that the crisis we have experienced was very real and extremely serious. We have made every possible effort to maximize the possibility of the talks process reconvening and to progress toward a settlement. When Republicans ran into problems in 1996, rather than making all efforts to salvage the situation, they played the "semtex card." We are not prepared to allow the difficulties we face from time to time to become levers for a return to conflict.

The UDP has consistently argued that the talks process must continue, and that the flaws must be addressed from within. Our position remains unaltered, despite the decision by the prisoners to withdraw their support. However, while we remain committed to see a continuation of the talks, opposition in our constituency is a matter for concern. It becomes a more significant obstacle if it affects the mood among the paramilitary leadership. In my view, this initial crumbling of support cannot be considered in isolation. If this warning signal is not dealt with, it could ultimately lead to a resumption of conflict. For, if lack of confidence grows to a level where the talks cannot take place, the ensuing vacuum will inevitably seduce the re-emergence of violence.

It is vital for confidence to be rebuilt where it has been eroded in order for the talks process to have any chance of success. In a few short weeks, the participants of the negotiations will have to face the most important and difficult decisions in the history of the conflict. It is at that point when it will become clear whether a political settlement will be achievable or not. It is unlikely that we will overcome that challenge while there is a serious lack of faith in the integrity of the peace process.

The UDP will be at Stormont tomorrow to continue its effort to bring peace to our society. We have not been diverted from the search for a democratic resolution of the conflict. However, it is important that we do not fool ourselves into believing that the continuation of the talks is equal to a removal of the potential danger. Stability must be introduced into this still volatile environment in order to encourage such political progress. I sincerely hope that the British government will take the necessary steps to redress the imbalance of its approach and direct its attention to rebuilding confidence within my community; otherwise, we may be only shunting the current crisis along ahead of us.

Sinn Féin in Double Bind

(*Ireland on Sunday* January 18, 1998)

Hypocrisy never seems to end...

One of the more amazing stories I saw this week was a newspaper report that Sinn Féin councilor Alex Maskey was going to take the Northern Ireland Office to court. To give a little background to the story, he was the first Sinn Féin representative to be included in the NIO key persons' scheme which supplies public representatives with security measures, such as bulletproof windows, panic alarms and the like.

Now one may have thought that this unprecedented move was the source of my interest, but no. What drew my attention was that Mr. Maskey refused to allow the RUC to inspect his home in order that it could be established what measures were necessary to protect his life. Instead, he insisted that a private firm should do the inspection. Apparently, he would not let the police near his house because he believed they might collude with Loyalists and thus actually threaten his safety. And, because the RUC are the only ones allowed to make security recommendations to the NIO, Mr. Maskey is taking them to court.

I was amazed. I would have thought the architects or the builders who would be doing the alterations would have had more reason to complain. It wasn't that long ago that Republicans considered these people to be legitimate targets, under the pretense that they were carrying out work for the security forces. The eight Protestants murdered at Teebane when the IRA blew up the minibus which was bringing them home, were employed by one of the firms which carries out most of the work in the key persons' scheme. Is it not a little hypocritical for Mr. Maskey to ask the British government to pay for his home to be secured, but to try to maintain his Republican credentials by refusing to let the police do their job? Incidentally, the decision on inclusion in the key persons' scheme depends on an RUC evaluation of potential risk to the person's safety. Of course, if he was attacked, I trust the first number he might dial would be 999.

Another example of Sinn Féin's doublespeak was more prevalent this week when the peace process took a leap forward. The initiative by the two governments in the form of a joint discussion document provided a catalyst that has resulted in the talks advancing to a new phase. This progress was warmly welcomed by Unionists and Nationalists alike. It is not often that you hear the same sentiments emerge from the mouths of David Trimble and John Hume. The only dissenting voice came from Sinn Féin, who warned the governments of the danger of retreating from agreed positions.

It struck me as peculiar for two reasons. Firstly, at every opportunity over the past two months I have listened intently to Gerry Adams lecture those of us around the negotiating table about the need for progress, and more emphatically that the governments must be the engine for such progress. Yet, Sinn Féin goes ballistic when they actually take the initiative. Secondly, I wondered what agreed positions Sinn Féin was talking about. Surely a joint document presented as the common view of both the British and Irish governments was in fact an agreed position. Perhaps it meant that the governments had moved from a previous position, and in many ways they have. But can this process achieve success if everyone maintains a rigid position? Absolutely not.

Clearly, the inference of Sinn Féin's comment was that the governments were retreating from a position previously agreed with Sinn Féin and, if that is the case, then I can't help wonder what exactly that agreement entailed and if it was the price for the latest IRA ceasefire. The question then is: what are the implications of Sinn Féin's warning?

If Republicans believe that they can press-gang the talks participants into a political arrangement contrary to the democratic will of the people, then they have learned nothing over the past thirty years. They refused to enter the peace process unless they were guaranteed that there would be no predetermined or precluded outcome. At the same time, they have remained single-minded and inflexible in their approach. Indeed, Mitchel McLaughlin said that Sinn Féin would oppose any settlement that involved partition. It is time that Republican doublespeak ended and we all got a clear indication of whether they are going to start engaging in this process in a serious and realistic manner.

UDP Actively and Irreversibly Opposed to the Use of Force

(*Ireland on Sunday* January 25, 1998)

On January 19, two INLA gunmen shot Loyalist Jim Guiney at his carpet show-room in Dunmurry. He was the eighth victim of the tit-for-tat killings following the death of Billy Wright.

The peace process has taken a grave turn, with the escalation of cyclical violence and the threat of IRA opposition to the talks. While I believe that the political difficulties at the talks can be resolved through the natural course of the negotiations, the spate of killings which has gripped the province threatens to bring the process to an abrupt end. The shootings have become a daily occurrence, and show no sign of abating. One of the victims was a friend of mine, Jim Guiney. He was brutally cut down by the INLA at the carpet shop that was his business. He left a wife and four children behind – another family destroyed by the conflict. This violence must not continue, for it serves no meaningful purpose.

The RUC Chief Constable has said that the UFF was involved in some way with three of the latest killings. That is in contrast to the UDP's information during the period under speculation. We are naturally taking his comments seriously, along with those that the IRA has been active under the cover-name of DAAD, shooting a man two weeks ago. If any of this is true, then it is a disturbing development. It is vital that none of the organizations that are on ceasefire become drawn into the fray by the opponents of the peace process. The INLA and LVF have kick-started the cycle of violence and are intent upon robbing the people of the opportunity of finding peace. The INLA murder of Jim Guiney was clearly calculated to widen the sphere of violence.

As a result of the speculation of UFF contravention of its

ceasefire, my party has come under extensive political pressure. Lord Alderdice has said that the UDP should be expelled from the talks process and should sever all links with paramilitary organizations. I want to make it clear that there is no question mark over the commitment of my party to the democratic process or our opposition to violence. The UDP is actively and irreversibly opposed to the use of force from any quarter.

That active opposition has led us to exert influence upon those who have traditionally supported the use of force and assist the transition of our society toward resolving its problems by democratic means. This is in sharp contrast to Lord Alderdice and his party. I am sick to the teeth of their sanctimonious attitude. They quickly come out in condemnation of violence, regardless of its origin, but then they retreat back to their comfortable homes, their conscience clear and certain that they have fulfilled their moral responsibility.

Meanwhile, members of my party have often put themselves in harms way, in an effort to change people's minds and diminish the potential for political violence. I am proud of the work that my colleagues have done over the years, despite adversity and personal risk, and of their continued efforts at this very difficult time to bring stability to the people of Northern Ireland. It angers me that our efforts are criticized by the Alliance Party or others, who have done nothing actively to prevent violence and whose condemnation has not saved a single life. If we fail at times, I apologize, but the UDP will not sever its links with the Loyalist paramilitaries; we will try even harder. If everyone took the same attitude as Lord Alderdice, there would never be an end to the conflict.

The transition from physical force to democracy cannot be made in one single leap. There will always be those who will resist or regress. Therefore, we must not give up in the face of this setback, but resolve to work harder to push the peace process back onto the rails. Exclusion from the negotiations would not enable us to do so. In fact, Seamus Mallon said earlier this week that if one party was forced from the talks, they would collapse. I agree with that assessment. Moreover, the destruction of the talks process will induce a full-scale emergence of conflict. The negotiations remain the only viable alternative to conflict. So, we must redouble our efforts to overcome the current crisis and enhance the determination to reach a political agreement.

The Voice of the UDP Must Be Heard at the Peace Talks

(*Ireland on Sunday* February 1, 1998)

On January 26, the UDP was expelled from the multi-party talks after the UFF's admission of involvement in the spate of tit-for-tat killings.

The exclusion of the UDP from the Northern Ireland talks is a serious setback for the peace process. The fewer parties that are at the table, the less comprehensive the negotiation process becomes, and, most importantly, less credible in the eyes of the public. Despite this setback, my party remains fundamentally committed to the process and will pursue an early re-entry with vigor.

The appalling spiral of violence which has gripped Northern Ireland poses a real threat. If it continues, it could rob the people of Northern Ireland of their last real hope of finding a political settlement. The statement by the LVF that it has modified its campaign could be construed as a step in the right direction but, ultimately, I want to see an unequivocal end to all political violence. The LVF, INLA and Continuity IRA should immediately cease their violence in order to maximize the potential for a political resolution of our problems.

The UDP has remained firm in its opposition to all violence. Ironically, it is directly because of our opposition to violence that we have been excluded from the talks. Were it not for our special relationship with the Ulster Freedom Fighters, the UDP would not have been considered by the governments to be culpable for that group's involvement in some of the recent violence. At the same time, if that relationship had not existed, the UFF would not have been convinced to bring its recent activity to an end, and in all likelihood there would not have been a Loyalist ceasefire in the first place.

That is the dilemma which faces the peace process for it is

not merely a process of democratic negotiation but also of conflict resolution. Paramilitary organizations are a component part of the conflict and must be incorporated into the resolution process. We cannot pretend that they do not exist, or that they are some form of alien species. They are part of the community and a product of our society's failure to resolve its differences through normal democratic devices. Paramilitary organizations must be encouraged to transform their view of the conflict, and they must be convinced that the way forward is not one articulated by violence. So who will assist them in that transition? The Alliance Party?

The UDP has built a relationship with one of those paramilitary organizations. Members of the UDP have gone to great lengths over a protracted period of time, sometimes putting themselves in danger, to persuade people who have traditionally expressed themselves through violence that the democratic process is the only legitimate vehicle for political expression. That transformation was never going to be a smooth one. We have seen the evidence of that, and the UDP has paid the price, but the UDP did not break the Mitchell Principles. My party has consistently voiced its opposition to all violence that has taken place.

The UFF were not the architects of the current spiral of inter-communal violence but were, nonetheless, unfortunately sucked into it. The UDP faced up to its responsibility, investigated the issue and, once UFF involvement was clear, we used our influence to urge the UFF to re-instate its ceasefire and come clean. Subsequently, their violence ended. Despite our actions, we have been punished. We would probably be in exactly the same circumstances today if we had decided to do nothing to end the violence.

Many people in Northern Ireland view the governments' decision as hypocritical. We have been ejected yet Sinn Féin remains at the talks, uncensored, despite the revelation by the RUC Chief Constable that the IRA has been militarily active. Indeed, it is more than clear that it shot a man in Belfast in a murder attempt earlier this month. The crucial difference is that the IRA never faced up to its responsibility.

It is widely believed that the IRA has been involved in Republican terrorist attacks, in particular the bombing of a hotel in Enniskillen at the weekend and an attempt to bomb Banbridge town center earlier this month. In that attack, the explosive technology bears all the hallmarks of the IRA and the detonator came from a batch procured by the IRA in 1989. Additionally, it is suspected that they are providing the INLA with intelligence information on Loyalists to assist that organization's murderous efforts.

The governments did not specify the timescale for the duration of our exclusion, but it has been suggested that it could last six weeks or more. That would effectively rule Loyalists out of the peace process as the final outcome of the negotiations must be agreed by May. If we are to be detached from those negotiations for the most part of the time remaining, we will have no influence upon the molding of the settlement at its most crucial stage. That would destroy any possibility of a comprehensive outcome of the talks.

A meeting with NIO officials took place on Friday to explore ways to overcome our exclusion. We hope that, as a result, the government will have recognized that our participation in the talks is in the best interest of the peace process and enhances the potential of its success. At a time when the LVF, INLA and others are on a mission to destroy the peace process, our exclusion only makes their task easier.

While we are dissatisfied with the handling of the issue, we do not reject the political process. Negotiations are the only way to resolve the conflict in Northern Ireland and heal the wounds of our divided society. Yet, for constructive negotiations to take place, the UDP must be included in order to fulfill its electoral mandate. Reconciliation, stability and peace can only be achieved through inclusiveness, and stability, in particular, can only be achieved by our speedy re-entry into the talks.

Sinn Féin Has Nothing to Fear from New Assembly

(*Ireland on Sunday* February 8, 1998)

While threats from the LVF continued to destabilize Northern Ireland, the negotiations finally moved toward substantive issues by discussing "sufficient consensus" and elections for a Northern Ireland Assembly.

This week John Hume said of Sinn Féin's attitude to a future Northern Ireland Assembly that it was "either being deliberately obstructive or failing to face reality." This stern attack by the SDLP is an indication of the crucial stage which the negotiation process has reached. It also identifies one of the major obstacles to be overcome if an agreement is to be reached.

While the talks have been in place since June 1996, it is only now that the real negotiations are taking place. I only wish I were there to take part. The crunch is finally approaching. The period of skirting around the core issues has ended and the time is near where actual agreement must be reached. Many people would say it's about time, but this is also the most challenging and precarious stage, when parties will have to move beyond their rhetoric. While shaping an accommodative settlement is difficult for each party in its own way, since everyone has to compromise on its public position, for some it is particularly difficult.

The peace process is one of conflict resolution, in which we must seek to overcome what are seemingly unbridgeable divisions and assist our people's transition from physical force to non-violent expression, and promote and sustain stability in our society. That process goes hand in hand with the political process which, through negotiation, must produce a political framework that can command the support and allegiance of all sections of the community.

If a political agreement can be reached, that should create the stability which can foster reconciliation and eventual resolution. Unfortunately, it is not immediately evident that such agreement will result from the current talks. It seems to me that Republicans may find the strain of accommodation unmanageable and, subsequently, that could lead to resumption of armed conflict and perpetual instability.

The level of compromise required for an accommodative settlement is not uniform to all parties, for all parties did not enter this process equidistant from the area of final agreement. Some have farther to travel than others, much farther. The negotiations must conform to democratic restraints, and as such the Republican ideological position is incompatible with what will be democratically acceptable. That is the core problem. All indications are that, despite the fact that Sinn Féin has shown some flexibility, it is having a real problem dealing with even the broad character of a realistic agreement. Its refusal to enter into any real discussion of a Northern Ireland Assembly characterizes that problem.

Every other participant accepts that the only logical and practical institutional arrangement for Northern Ireland is an Assembly. The only real scope of negotiation is the extent of its power, its operational structure and its relationship with other bodies. Republicans refuse to accept this reality and continue to churn out their ideological position of an Irish unitary state, despite the fact that every other party has moved on from there. Until Sinn Féin gets into the same ball-park as everyone else, there are likely to be real problems ahead.

It is interesting that Unionism is under constant and intense attack from Republicans for not "getting real," while at the same time Sinn Féin hides behind smoke-screens of lack of engagement and internal settlements. Republicans keep on insisting that the status quo is not an option, when the real issue is whether Sinn Féin has the capacity to face a realistic political agreement. Unionists are not, through subterfuge, trying to invoke some form of return to the old Stormont, the bogie man that Republicans raise to avoid the real political debate. It is not a devious ploy to put Nationalism down, but rather a genuine effort to create acceptable political structures that allow Unionists and Nationalists to share their future.

I recognize that, for a political arrangement to be workable, it must conform not only to the parameters of what is democratically acceptable, which means acceptable to both Unionists and Nationalists, but also accommodate the needs for expression of identity of both sections of the community. There is no continuation of the status quo, or internal settlement. If Sinn Féin equates the status quo with continued partition, then, yes, they are correct, because Northern Ireland will remain part of the United Kingdom. There is no consent for any other option; but neither is there consent for a continuation of an undemocratic system of governance. Agreed structures must be innovative and the settlement comprehensive, spanning the totality of relationships throughout these Isles. The key to the success of a new Northern Ireland Assembly will be in its character. It must be based on the principles of consent and co-determination, incorporating proportional representation, a bill of rights, a written constitution, and accountable and democratic government.

There is nothing to fear from such an institution for it will be based on the consent of both Unionists and Nationalists. That is not a return to Stormont, but a new beginning in which the people of Northern Ireland, despite their differences, can work together in their collective interest and, for the first time, co-determine their future. It is time that Sinn Féin faces up to the reality of a new settlement, and recognizes that the need for fundamental change is something it must apply to its own rigid position. Republicans must shed their ideological straitjacket and broaden their vision. They must embrace the opportunity for our divided people to build a new Northern Ireland based on accountability, fairness and equality as the cornerstone of a new set of relationships throughout these Isles.

Clear Evidence that IRA Ceasefire Is Over Cannot Be Ignored

(*Ireland on Sunday* February 15, 1998)

The killings of Brendan Campbell on February 9 and Robert Dougan on February 10 led to further speculation of IRA involvement in the recent spate of violence, thus challenging Sinn Féin's position at the negotiating table.

Sinn Féin is likely to face serious pressure when the talks open in Dublin tomorrow. The clear indication that the IRA murdered two men within twenty-four hours earlier this week cannot be ignored. If the governments choose to ignore the increasing evidence, they will be guilty of applying double standards and of protecting the Provos.

Sinn Féin, of course, says this has nothing to do with them and they don't speak for anyone but themselves. That, however, does not cut much ice anywhere on this island. In fact, it's a little insulting that they should still be trying to pull that one and be so blatantly dishonest about their relationship with the IRA and the undeniable fact that their relevance to the peace process goes far beyond the size of their electoral mandate. The IRA's suggestion that the ceasefire is intact is nothing more than an ill-disguised scam to cloud the waters in Sinn Féin's favor when they face questions tomorrow.

The truth behind the pseudonym Direct Action Against Drugs is well established. DAAD was created in 1995 to provide the IRA with a cover to protect their decision to move against a series of drug dealers while on ceasefire, partly in order to protect their own interests in that trade. They killed eight men over a period of months and then ended the campaign when the security forces started to get too close and public tolerance began to wear thin. Sir Hugh Annesley, the RUC Chief Constable at that time, publicly acknowledged that DAAD and the IRA were one and the same. This was confirmed by political figures both in the UK and Ireland.

Brendan (Bap) Campbell is DAAD's ninth victim. A major drug dealer, he had been a target of the IRA for some time. They tried to murder him two years ago during the first set of DAAD murders, and their intent deepened when he began thumbing his nose at them. It was widely published that he lobbed two grenades at Connolly House, Sinn Féin's headquarters, not long ago, and phoned them up to let them know that it was he. Not the brightest move in his position, I would have thought. Subsequently, the IRA shot him twice in the chest at the Three Meadows pub in Belfast last month. He survived because he was wearing a bullet-proof vest. On Monday night, however, they caught up with him and finished the job, also seriously injuring his lady friend.

Ronnie Flanagan, the current Chief Constable, acknowledged three weeks ago that he believed DAAD had wounded Campbell in the previous shooting, and referred to the IRA as being active. Earlier this week, Taoiseach Bertie Ahern confirmed that he understood DAAD to be responsible for murdering Campbell and that DAAD was the IRA. If the noose was slowly tightening around Sinn Féin's neck, it was given a sharp tug when the IRA murdered Bobby Dougan the next day. He was shot dead as he sat in his car in Dunmurry. The car used by the gunmen was abandoned in Twinbrook Estate in a carbon copy of the murder of Jim Guiney, who was killed three weeks before, less than one hundred yards away. Three IRA suspects were allegedly seen running from the getaway car and were arrested in a flat a short time later, following a tip-off to the police. The INLA then released a categorical denial of any involvement in Mr. Dougan's murder, firmly directing attention toward the Provos. The IRA made no rebuttal.

Ronnie Flanagan has now publicly stated what we already know: that the IRA killed these two men. It is my conviction that the IRA ceasefire is over and that the sanction for these attacks came from the highest levels of the Republican movement. There is other evidence, which I cannot elaborate upon, but I believe it will become clear in good time. I fully expect that there will be further Republican attacks upon Loyalists in the coming weeks. A number of Loyalists, including members of the UDP, have been warned that they are being targeted by Republicans and there is a campaign of malevolent gossip being circulated by Sinn Féin about some Loyalist political figures with a view to justify future IRA action.

The IRA could have exonerated the public end of its cease-fire in the context of continued Loyalist attacks on the Nationalist community. But, when Loyalist violence ended some weeks ago, that option was removed. Therefore, Republicans have been forced to manufacture that phenomenon themselves. I believe that the IRA murdered Bobby Dougan specifically to encourage a Loyalist response, for the purpose of creating an escape route for the IRA from the peace process. Consequently, I appeal to Loyalists to recognize Republican intentions and not be manipulated into performing a role devised for them by others.

None of this bodes well, for it appears that the IRA has decided there is no future in the talks process and this is the first step of its exit strategy. I hope I am paranoid and wrong in this case. Only time will tell. But, in the meantime, the governments have no choice but to be seen to act accordingly tomorrow and apply the rules to Sinn Féin as they did to the UDP three weeks ago. If they don't, then the integrity of the process and the impartiality of each government will be in question. We do not want to see anyone excluded from the talks, but we did not create the rules and there must be consistency in their application.

Sinn Féin Expulsion Is Fair
(*Irish Voice* February 18–24, 1998)

After security sources claimed that there was ballistic evidence linking the IRA to Brendan Campbell's murder, and ballistic as well as forensic evidence linking it to the killing of Robert Dougan, calls for Sinn Féin's expulsion from the talks were voiced. Sinn Féin responded by saying that it would challenge any attempt to be ejected as "Sinn Féin was not involved in the killing of anyone."

With the prospect of Sinn Féin being suspended from the talks process, following a number of IRA murders, commentators are questioning whether the talks process can survive. Despite the contention that the talks would not be viable without Sinn Féin, the mechanics of the process allow the talks to continue without them or indeed the UDP. The remaining parties constitute a majority of both the Unionist and Nationalist electorate and therefore decisions can be taken and conceivably an agreement could be reached and subsequently endorsed at referendum.

The question, however, which should be asked is whether the talks have any point without Sinn Féin and the UDP, for the prospect of a successful outcome does depend to some extent on inclusiveness and stability. Already, a significant minority of Unionism has absented itself from the talks voluntarily. The DUP and UKUP withdrew last year and have vowed to oppose whatever comes out of the talks at referendum. My own party is currently under suspension and now the exit of Sinn Féin means that a sizable part of the overall Northern Ireland electorate is not represented at the peace talks for one reason or another. The process is inevitably weakened by the lack of inclusiveness. The more parties are outside, the less comprehensive the developing agreement becomes, and the more difficult it will be to sell since there are fewer fingerprints discernible on the package.

While the absence of the DUP and UKUP cannot be redressed as it is by their own choice, the UDP and Sinn Féin do not face indefinite exclusion. But that is little comfort at this vital stage of the talks, when the crunch issues are being addressed. Many of you may well think that neither the UDP nor Sinn Féin should have been suspended from the talks in the first place and that it makes more sense to have everyone at the table and to talk the problems out. Of course, I would agree. In other conflict resolution processes throughout the world, that may have transpired, for it is uncommon for transition from physical force to democratic agreement to be swift and clean. There will always be incidents of violence along the way to remind divided societies of the difficult task upon which they have embarked. But, equally, the process itself must be fair to all participants; indeed, more importantly, it must be seen to be fair.

The suspension of the UDP last month, which, incidentally, was advocated by Sinn Féin, has set a precedent which must now be followed. If the IRA were to get away with murders while the UDP was hoisted over Loyalist violence, the community at large would interpret the process as being tilted in favor of Republicans. I believe that it was wrong for my party to be excluded but, if the rules are applied to us, it would be disastrous for them not to be applied also to Sinn Féin.

I think it is unfortunate and unhelpful that Sinn Féin is still engaged in what was described by political advisor and commentator Fergus Finlay as "a polite deceit." The constant denial that Sinn Féin has no linkage with the IRA may suit the purposes of deflecting culpability for the IRA's actions, but, overall, I believe it does not wear well in the eyes of most people, for it is seen as tactical dishonesty. If Sinn Féin's relevance stretched no further than its electoral mandate, why is it so important for Sinn Féin to be part of the process at all, since larger parties are already on the outside? Why was Sinn Féin not permitted to join the talks in the first place because of the IRA campaign of violence, if there was no connection? And why did Sinn Féin choose not to contest that point legally then, when it would have been more appropriate to do so?

I could write ten articles about this single point, but there is no point, for you all know what I'm getting at. Let's have some honesty and integrity about who represents whom and why! It would send an altogether negative message if Sinn Féin were let off the hook because it is able to hide behind the smokescreen about its relationship with the IRA, while my party, which has taken a stronger public position against violence, is chucked out because it has been consistently honest about its position.

What is important is that we get over this rump, Sinn Féin takes its medicine, and that we move forward in an atmosphere free from violence. The instability that results from continued violence has already had a profoundly negative effect on the chances for a positive outcome of this process. The rapprochement necessary between the communities in Northern Ireland is hampered by the fact that we are still killing each other. Both Protestants and Catholics have lost their lives at the hands of activists from the other community. If this violence continues, then it threatens to engulf our society in a whirlwind of terror which will destroy the peace process.

Sinn Féin leaders have warned that their expulsion could signal an end of the peace process and many interpret that as a threat that the IRA will return to a full-scale terrorist campaign. It has already ended its ceasefire by murdering two men last week, resulting in Sinn Féin's current dilemma. The IRA has fostered uncertainty by indicating that its ceasefire is intact, while not suggesting that it is unbreached. That could have been a ploy to provide some political cover for Sinn Féin, or an indication that it had employed violence in a measured and managed way. In either case, it keeps everyone guessing what its next step will be.

Following the lapse in the UFF cessation last month, Loyalists clarified their position, outlining that their actions were retaliatory responses to Republican violence, and then fully restoring the UFF ceasefire. The IRA must come clean and admit its actions and reinstate its cessation; otherwise, it must be assumed that more IRA violence will come. That paints a very gloomy picture indeed, and the implications are distinct. If Republicans recognize those implications, then the peace process may be salvageable. If they do not recognize them or perhaps do not care, then their violence could quickly place the situation out of control and beyond all of our reaches.

UDP Blueprint for North–South Rapprochement

(*Ireland on Sunday* February 22, 1998)

As the UDP prepared for re-entering the talks, Sinn Féin was expelled from the negotiations following IRA involvement in the Campbell and Dougan murders.

The talks were in Dublin for three days last week. Yet, because of the controversy over Sinn Féin's participation as a result of IRA murders, not one single word of negotiation took place on the original agenda issue – North–South relationships. But the talks will return to this issue soon enough, especially since Northern Ireland's relationship with the Republic of Ireland is the bugbear for Unionism just like the Assembly is the most contentious aspect for Nationalism.

Each party is going to judge the outcome of the negotiations in the context of the overall package. And the road toward agreement is a three stranded one, meaning that, while intricate negotiation is taking place on each of the strands in its own right, a careful eye remains on the overall progress across the strands. The SDLP does not want to take decisions on an Assembly until it can see how strand two is shaping up and vice versa for Unionism. It is clear that no party will be able to point to an emerging agreement as a fulfillment of its own agenda. It is equally clear that any agreement needs to reflect sufficiently each community's needs. Yet, it would be wrong to believe that an agreement can be reached on the basis of a simple trade-off between Unionism and Nationalism on strands one and two.

Loyalists are prepared to work toward an accommodative settlement creating structures across the three strands that can command the support and allegiance of both traditions. The construction of such a settlement, however, depends upon the recognition of practical parameters. That means that the debate on North–South structures must be driven by what is actually possible and desirable as opposed to being an elaborate quid pro quo for Nationalists because of the creation of an Assembly.

The UDP is not opposed in principle to cooperative relationships between the jurisdictions, provided it makes sense economically and that it is part of broader regional cooperation throughout the British Isles. There is no consent for any model based on the Framework Document, which we consider to be deterministic and asymmetrical, failing to address the totality of relationships in a genuine manner. The territorial claim over Northern Ireland is an obvious hindrance to developing a more constructive relationship between our jurisdictions but, if that is satisfactorily addressed, greater possibilities do exist.

As we see it, the potential development of cross-border structures comprises two components: firstly, that deeper economic and business links between Northern Ireland and the Republic will be economically beneficial, and secondly, that cross-border cooperation may encourage reconciliation between Nationalists and Unionists. Both components are limited by the economic and political parameters on the ground. Indeed, there are economic, practical, and political obstacles to greater cooperation, but that does not mean that such cooperation should not exist. It merely serves to limit the scope of and expectations for North–South structures in accordance with economic reality.

The Framework Document sought to develop a North–South focus. The position of Northern Ireland within the United Kingdom, however, as well as the UK's and Irish Republic's economic and political orientation within Europe, makes it clear that comprehensive cooperation fully embracing the totality of relationships can only take place on a British Isles wide basis. We envisage that, in some areas of public policy, it may be mutually beneficial to expand cooperation. These include transport, infrastructure, agriculture and fisheries, health, the environment, tourism, anti-drugs, smuggling, labor law, unemployment, EU programs, education and training, industrial and trade matters, waterways, social welfare, and energy. This would be part of a wider cooperation on these issues as is appropriate between other regions.

We also see the North–South component of cooperation being structured by a Ministerial Council which will bring together ministers from the Northern Ireland Assembly and the Irish Parliament to explore issues of mutual concern and advise the respective legislatures on proposals for their approval. Nevertheless, it is a matter of a central nature that executive authority should remain with the respective seats of power in order to prevent administrative and legislative conflict, as well as to ensure that North–South structures are not an attempt at "rolling integration" into a united Ireland. At the same time, North–South cooperation would strengthen the political stability of Northern Ireland by providing Nationalism with an institutional expression of identity.

Parades: They Haven't Gone Away, You Know

(*Ireland on Sunday* March 1,1998)

The Northern Ireland Office appointed two new members to the Parades Commission, Glen Barr and Tommy Cheevers. The Loyalist background of both provoked Nationalist criticism of the Commission and the appointments.

Earlier this week, there was some controversy over the new members of the Parades Commission. You're probably saying – Oh God. Not parades! – but we will be immersed in the issue of contentious marches again very shortly. As they say – it hasn't gone away, you know! Anyway, the remodeling of Parades Commission personnel has got the ball rolling on the annual parades debate, so I thought I would get in early.

Glen Barr and Tommy Cheevers are both community workers with experience of dealing with cross-community issues. But their new role on the Parades Commission has caused a bit of a stir because of their backgrounds. Barr used to be a leading member of the UDA and a political activist twenty years ago; Cheevers is a current member of the Apprentice Boys.

Some Nationalists have criticized their appointment, citing their respective backgrounds as evidence that they cannot be impartial or objective. Some Unionists have questioned their choice to serve on a Commission that has little credibility in the eyes of the Unionist community. I suppose you could argue in a perverse way that they may be ideal choices since they have provoked a balanced, if negative, reaction from both sections of the community. One thing for sure is that they have taken on a role which will earn them very little in the way of favor or advancement. Although the hefty salary which accompanies the position may help relieve their discomfort, people have not exactly been queuing up for the jobs. Personally, I would not take that job for a pension, and not just because it seems like political suicide. Its lack of credibility is so far gone that it is impossible to visualize how it will make any meaningful contribution toward resolving disputes.

Nationalist critics want to know why the Secretary of State chose to put an Apprentice Boy on the body. In their view, this has distorted the Commission because there is no corresponding place for someone related to the residents' groups which oppose parades. I think they have got a point there. While I do not think Mr. Cheevers was selected just because he is an Apprentice Boy, he would be able to bring an aspect of local knowledge to the workings of a body that has been panned for not really understanding the complexities of the problem. If the Commission thought that was a valuable fringe benefit, it would make sense that the same qualities in a Nationalist representative would be a positive contribution as well.

But, that aside, no amount of tinkering with the Commission's membership is going to make it an effective instrument for resolving the parades problem. The only real success story in its short history was the intervention in Newtownbutler that resulted in an uneasy peace between the two sides, at least for a time. The Reverend Roy Magee mediated in that instance, succeeding where others had failed because he was seen as someone who knew the score and was able to gain the trust of both factions. But he resigned from the Commission because he saw that its role was being modified to take the emphasis of power away from mediation and toward adjudication. He knew at that point that it was a defunct entity.

To believe that the parades problem can be overcome by a Commission which behaves not unlike a tribunal, ruling on parade disputes, is lunacy. Surely, the objective must be to attempt to resolve local parades at a grassroots level and foster understanding or compromise which would prevent a Parades Commission from having to rule on the damn thing at all. If a contentious parade finds itself in the hands of the Commission in the first place, the resolution process has already failed.

Transferring the ultimate decision on individual parades from the RUC to the Parades Commission may shift the blame but it won't stop confrontation. Whoever decides, it is still the RUC who have to police the decision and who will find themselves between the warring factions. I believe that the Parades Commission is a waste of time and money. Its existence is nothing more than an attempt by the government to be seen to be doing something about the issue and an attempt to take the blame for decisions out of the hands of the RUC.

The shape it has taken since it was created has justified concerns about its ability to make any genuine contribution to overcoming the parades dilemma. Throwing money at the Commission or making adjustments to its make-up won't do anything to reverse that lack of credibility. The people who have chosen to serve on it may well be genuine people full of good intentions but, unless the problem is addressed at the grassroots level through mediation between opposing groups, there will not be any resolution. The Parades Commission has decided to take a different route and those people should consider whether there is any point to their continued participation in a body which has nothing to offer.

Unpopular Decision Must Be Made for Sake of Peace
(*Ireland on Sunday* March 8, 1998)

On March 3, two life-long friends, Catholic Damien Trainor and Protestant Philip Allen, were shot dead by the LVF in a pub in the village of Poyntzpass, County Armagh.

Poyntzpass. Until this week it was a place I had heard little of. I've never been through it, and probably could not accurately locate it on a map. I am aware of its existence only because it is marked on the train schedules. A sleepy little village, it seems to have been a place apart during the Troubles, where the divisions that have shredded our society didn't really feature at all. A place that, until now, time and the conflict appeared to have forgotten.

Now everyone knows of Poyntzpass. It has joined the catalogue of towns and villages that have become nameplates on the roll of honor of Northern Ireland's atrocities – Enniskillen, Loughinisland, Teebane, Darkley, Warrenpoint, Ballygawley, and now Poyntzpass. The human consequences of this double murder are truly tragic, but the circumstances of the atrocity have a political resonance that has not been missed. The deaths of the two young men at Poyntzpass have taken on a symbolic significance because one was Catholic and one was Protestant, both firm friends – a relationship that stretched across the religious divide. Two families from different traditions united in shared grief are seen to articulate the message that violence damages the entire community.

The government, media and politicians have knowingly exploited that characteristic of this horrific attack to its full worth. The nature of these murders has become a powerful tool. Every ounce of propaganda has been milked out of this tragedy and heaped onto those responsible in an effort to smother what credibility they still have with the public. They need not have bothered, for the impact of these killings struck home instinctively to a society which has seen it all before. After the series of hammerblows it has endured this year, it is clearly saying that it has had enough.

Northern Ireland has experienced more than three-and-a-half thousand murders and tens of thousands of bombings. Each is tragic in its own right. And each time, when people lose their lives or when towns are destroyed by bombs, we hear words insisting that we must plow ahead and that the violence only strengthens our resolve, and similar predictable phrases which are ultimately meaningless. I know because I have done so along with every other politician at some time, the sentiments genuine but knowing there is little hope of breaking the cycle. But now things are different.

For the first and perhaps last time, the chance of a settlement, that elusive goal, is actually within our collective grasp. We can allow ourselves to be subsumed by the treadmill of violence and once again learn to live with it as we have done for nearly three decades. Or we can pool our energy toward making that last effort to drag ourselves out of the mire. I have seen real opportunity emerge in the past few weeks at the talks, and I believe that a political agreement is possible, if the determination is there. On the street, I sense exasperation among the ordinary folk who are trying unsuccessfully to square my talk of hope with the visual reality of towns devastated by car-bombs and lives stolen by bullets. And emotionally, for society as a whole, it *is* hard to equate the two. Yet, when I am in that negotiating room, I can sense the opportunity that's there, and I look at those who are detonating bombs and know that it is a desperate sign of their own failure.

The closer we move toward agreement at the talks the more desperate the efforts of those who oppose progress will become. In all likelihood, there will be more bombs and perhaps more deaths. But, if we become unfocused now, then we may as well jack it in, because this chance is not going to come around again. The hardest choices any of us will ever make will be made over the next few weeks in a stuffy room at Stormont. They are not choices one longs for and some may not be prepared to meet that challenge and may cut and run. Perhaps some are already moving that way, but the UDP has not lost its determination to face up to the challenge. If political courage is shown among the parties at the talks, and the community can see a real determination to put our shoulders to the grindstone, then I believe that there can be a political agreement which will be supported by the people. The oxygen that the opponents of peace in our society need to survive will be extinguished.

Day that Symbolizes a Self-Imposed Cultural Apartheid

(*Ireland on Sunday* March 15, 1998)

The time of the annual White House St. Patrick's Day reception has once again arrived.

As I write this column, I am crossing the Atlantic on my way to New York, where I am spending a few days before traveling to Washington for the St. Patrick's Day function at the White House. The event has a political importance which demands my presence. About three hundred other souls travel with me and, throughout the cabin, there is a lot of craic with a group of women in the compartment behind singing their hearts out and a lot of laughter and good-natured banter echoing all around. The flight is chock-full as is to be expected at this time of year when thousands find their way out of Ireland to the cities of New York and Boston, where they will live it up in a land that St. Patrick never visited. They will be celebrating a part of their culture and history with people, most of whom have never been to Ireland but behave like they are more Irish than the Irish themselves. The New York parade is legendary but I have never gone to watch it because I cannot identify with its exaggeration of Irishness and reputation for being a platform for Republican sympathy groups.

It's all alien to me, for St. Patrick's Day does not feature high on the calendar of events within the Protestant community. Like so many other areas of history and culture, it has become politicized and identified with one section of the community. The religious and ideological divisions in Ireland have been consolidated over time with a self-imposed cultural apartheid. Rather than nurturing our combined cultural wealth, our society has preoccupied itself with dividing up the pot. We have bastardized our heritage and used it as an instrument to accentuate separateness, despite the fact that most of our traditions and mythical folklore predate the emergence of our current division and even Christianity itself.

In Lisburn, where I live, there is no St. Patrick's Day celebration. The shops do not shut and businesses do not close, except of course the banks. They are obliged to do so since it is a recognized bank holiday. But, other than that, the cultural significance of St. Patrick's Day does not intrude upon life in Lisburn. That is not unusual, for celebrations only take place in largely Nationalist areas of the province. For instance, I drove through Downpatrick last weekend and was not surprised to find numerous banners stretched across the main roads advertizing the St. Patrick's Day parade. After all, if any place should rightly celebrate St. Patrick, it's Downpatrick. But what caught my eye was the fact that the banner advertized the event as Downpatrick's "cross-community" St. Patrick's Day parade. That said it all. If there was ever evidence of how our heritage has been so fundamentally corrupted, it was there on those banners, upon which Downpatrick District Council felt compelled to point out the novelty of their parade.

Once an area of cultural identity is allowed to become solely synonymous with one tradition, it is extremely difficult to redress that problem. Such is the case with St. Patrick's Day. This year is the first that Belfast City Council has ventured to organize a celebration and some controversy has surrounded the prospect, with division emerging about whether it should happen at all, followed by debate on the make up of the management group. It is unlikely that the Belfast parade will boast many participants from the Protestant tradition, as the Shankill Partnership, for example, declined to contribute because of lack of preparation time and concern that the organizers comprised almost solely Nationalist groups. Cultural and political sensitivities demand that there is no feeling of alienation among Protestants surrounding this venture and that it is seen to be a shared project. Perhaps the perceptions, which have dogged the parade this year, can be overcome for next year's event and the current difficulties can then be written off as teething problems.

I think it is important that we attempt to reverse the ingrained tendency for separateness within our society. We need to encourage people to explore each other's sense of culture, history and identity for, upon scrutiny, we may find that it is not so alien to us and the commonality we share will emerge. I long for the day when we will not have two separate Irish History curricula in Northern Ireland's schools, where there is not an instinctive recoil from the promotion of the Irish language's place in our history, or aggression against the expression of Orange culture. It is important that our society learns not only to re-examine each of our selective interpretations of history and culture, but also to learn to tolerate and perhaps understand each other's sense of identity and maybe even reach out to share aspects of culture. Indeed, I wonder how St. Patrick would feel, looking down on us and seeing division so strong that we cannot even come together to celebrate his rich contribution to our history. That he as the patron saint of Ireland has become exploited as an instrument of our division. I'm sure he would not be at all impressed by our demonstration of Christianity.

Paisley's "Dinosaurs" Are an Obstacle to Peace

(*Irish Voice* 25–31 March, 1998)

On March 19, police were called to a DUP anti-peace process rally in Lisburn where heated exchanges between the DUP and UDP were taking place.

The past week has certainly been an eventful one, for me at least. I came face to face with opponents from my community on Thursday night at a DUP rally in Lisburn, my home town. It showed me that there are significant elements prepared to go to any length to prevent intelligent debate. These people will firmly resist any form of political evolution in our society.

Ian Paisley organized what had been described as a Unionist meeting at Lisburn Orange Hall. Curiously, the only "Unionists" who participated in this public event were the leaders of his party. The UK Unionist leader Bob McCartney and Ulster Unionist MP Jeffrey Donaldson had allegedly been invited and refused to take part. They obviously knew that it would just be a DUP grandstanding exercise.

My party was not invited and it was clear that we were not welcome, despite – or should I say because of – the fact that I am the leader of a political party with a significant role in the peace process. I am also a councilor for the district in which the meeting took place. Therefore, I thought it was my right to attend the meeting, along with my Lisburn Council colleague David Adams, to add our view to the debate. Debate, however, was the last thing on the DUP's mind. For, as soon as the meeting began, they branded us from the platform as opponents of the DUP, troublemakers, and threatened to have us removed by the RUC.

I tried to speak from the floor and ask why I, as a Unionist, was not allowed to make a contribution, and was being excluded from the meeting by the organizers. I was shouted down and intimidated by the people on the platform, and by their supporters in the room, most of whom had Ulsterbus coaches waiting outside to spirit them to their homes, far from Lisburn. One of my party members was attacked and struck on the back of the head by a DUP supporter as we left the room, having failed to have our say. That brought home to me the obstacles we face as Unionists in trying to bring a durable peace settlement to the people of Northern Ireland.

My colleagues and I had just spent six days in New York and Washington DC fulfilling a series of political and social engagements. The climax was a private meeting with Bill Clinton in the Oval Office, the first such meeting between Ulster Loyalists and the President. This was a reflection of the significance attached to the current, crucial stage of the peace process. There appears to be a great anticipation in the United States that a settlement will emerge over the next few weeks. This, coupled with the traditional vibrancy of the St. Patrick's Day celebrations, seemed to produce an air of euphoria. I had to do my best to prevent people running away with the idea that a deal is inevitable. Most of the political parties involved in the talks were in the States, and that may have contributed to the sense of positive electricity. But the fact that we were all over there, while there is still so much work to be concluded at home, should not have been interpreted as meaning that we exuded the confidence of success.

I believe there can be a political agreement. But that, of course, depends on the others in the peace talks as well. I believe they too can sense the emergence of an agreement. The challenge will be whether we can put that down on paper and then, more importantly, have the strength to endorse it publicly. That's going to be the problem. Most intelligent people can interpret the broad parameters of a democratically acceptable agreement. Any sensible person who has lived through the Troubles can frame in his or her own mind the limits of compromise. You don't have to be a politician to do that. The difficulty, however, is translating that into something solid and tangible. That, for all political leaders, is the dilemma of putting thought into practice. It is a particular strain if one is expected to do so in the faith that it will be accurately interpreted by one's own constituency, and not distorted by opponents. It is a risky business, for sure, especially when you look at the nature of the opposition that some of us have to confront.

There are dinosaurs and delusionists on both sides – people who have failed to evolve with the changing world and who remain cocooned in the rhetoric and idealism of a previous century. I despair because these people still fail to recognize the need for transition in our society, and are prepared to hold us all hostage to the inevitability of conflict, which is the companion of mutual intransigence. These people will poison society with conspiracy theories and black propaganda, fueling uncertainty and fear in communities which are already nervous. They do so in an effort to undermine the chance of either reaching an agreement or selling it to the people.

I think that, if the parties have courage, they can reach a political agreement. But it is unlikely that all those in the talks will physically endorse the outcome, though I hope they will not oppose it. Sinn Féin, for example, is restricted ideologically from endorsing structures that will be agreed. And this brings me to my main point: if we somehow manage to overcome the multitude of hurdles we face at the talks in the next few weeks, the agreement that will emerge should not be mistaken as a settlement. The agreement is only the creation of mechanisms through which we can pursue stability and encourage long-term reconciliation by bridging the divide between the communities. That is going to take some time.

Those in the DUP who oppose the peace process, and those in Sinn Féin who are likely to oppose the structures, will be active either inside or outside those institutions of governance. Let's not pin all our hopes on the illusion that agreement at the talks will erase division. Success at the talks is only the next logical stage in a much longer settlement process.

Constitutional Changes Are a Must if Peace Is to Be Found

(*Ireland on Sunday* March 29, 1998)

On March 23, the multi-party negotiations at Stormont resumed after the annual trek of most Northern Irish parties to Washington for St. Patrick's Day. With the Easter deadline looming in the background, there even seemed to have been some movement in the Unionist position toward North–South relations and in the Republican position toward increased commitment to the process, with all its implications.

The negotiations have been intensified and, if the courage and determination are there, an agreement will emerge from the talks before Easter. That means that all the difficult issues which have not yet been agreed will have to be resolved satisfactorily. One of the issues that has produced controversy in the Republic of Ireland is the prospect of constitutional change as part of the overall political settlement. Sinn Féin continues to argue in the talks that there should be no change to the constitution of the Republic, while we, as Unionists, insist that it is a central part of the package.

I assume that views are mixed in the Republic about this matter, but I hope that people will acknowledge that it is impossible for Unionists to accept any proposals that fail to address the claim over the territory of Northern Ireland. If we are to learn to coexist in peace on this island, then such inflammatory and aggressive legislation cannot remain. Further, I do not interpret an agreement on new relationships to be a transitional arrangement, but the model for an eventual settlement, creating political structures which can command the support and confidence of all the people of Northern Ireland. The maintenance of a constitutional imperative which provides the justification for Republican aggression in Northern Ireland and provokes a hostile view of the Republic within

Unionism is not compatible with what this process is designed to achieve.

The government of the Republic of Ireland has made a firm and irreversible commitment to change offensive sections of its constitution and I welcome that as a positive contribution to the search for a fair settlement. It is vital that no ambiguity surrounds the constitutional status of Northern Ireland as a separate entity. I, however, am sensitive to some of the concerns and misapprehensions within Nationalism in Northern Ireland and within society in the Republic about the effect of such changes. I did a talk show in Washington the other week and Paul Hill was a guest. He outlined his opposition to changes in Articles Two and Three, stating that Nationalists could not accept any measure that took away their Irish identity and prevented Northern Nationalists from holding Irish passports. I could not believe my ears.

The necessary constitutional changes have nothing whatsoever to do with subjugating the right of identity of those in Northern Ireland who consider themselves Irish, nor does it represent any infringement on their rights to express that identity. This process is not about Unionists banning Irish passports or trying to convert Nationalists into British people. Indeed, the opposite is true. I feel that the removal of offensive legislation will encourage greater tolerance for our differing senses of identity and a more neutral political environment.

I expect that changes will reflect the legitimacy of aspirations of unity, aspirations which can be pursued democratically and which are subject to the right of the people of Northern Ireland to determine their own future. I would encourage those who continue to hold a fundamental opposition to changes in the Irish constitution to consider whether they are prepared to ruin the opportunities for building a peaceful settlement in Northern Ireland. An obstinate refusal to replace outdated and inappropriate legislation with more democratic principles is symptomatic of the failure to transcend the traditional conflict in pursuit of new relationships, which are consistent with the evolving social values and the experiences of global change.

Would it not be ridiculous for the people of the Republic of Ireland to reject the propositions presented to them at referendum, which would provide the basis for peace throughout our islands, simply because of an objection to changes to a constitution which has proved unenforceable anyhow? The changes to Articles Two and Three will happen. It has already been accepted that they will be part of the overall agreement, and we merely have to negotiate the wording of those changes. It is important that the potential for a political agreement is not obstructed by a refusal to change Articles Two and Three at the referendum. If that were to happen, what kind of message would it send to people in my community?

The Heat Is On – NI Talks Deadline Looms

(*Irish Voice* April 1-7, 1998)

On March 25, talks chairman George Mitchell set the deadline for reaching a peace settlement for April 9. Opponents to the process reacted by increasing their attempts to derail the negotiations. On March 29, a former RUC officer was shot by Republicans as he left a supermarket.

Nine days to go! Nine days to overcome divisions which span centuries. Can we do it? The question should be: can we afford to fail? By Easter, the talks process will have either produced an agreement or it will have confirmed the intractability of our differences. Personally, I think we can make it come good, or at least as good as it is likely to get. For, if there is to be success, everyone around the table will have to accept that there are areas in the negotiations that will not go in their favor.

Some hopeless aspirations still dog the discussions. Decommissioning, for one, has been a bugbear of the entire process, and has had its ugly head raised once again in the past two weeks by the Ulster Unionists. I can empathize with the strains they may be experiencing within their constituency at the non-materialization of weapons of war, but that is one of the pressure points which will not be successfully relieved, at least not in the foreseeable future.

It is clear that, while for a good many people in Northern Ireland the desire to see the removal of illegal weapons is felt strongly because of increasing violence, it is actually less likely to occur now than before. This is simply because it is not those who are committed to the success of the peace process who are waging the conflict now, but its opponents. These groups are therefore beyond the influence or control of anyone within the talks.

The organizations currently on ceasefire are also not likely to disarm. They are keeping a careful eye on the malcontents in the other community who are trying to induce war. Those malcontents are, no doubt, wary of their counterparts who are at present committed to the process, but who they are not convinced will remain so indefinitely. That is the character of the conflict and, more specifically, the conflict resolution process. The trust which is required to allow universal disarmament will take much more time. The Unionist Party will have to live with that for the time being. But, at the same time, we must not ignore the issue, for the resolution process will not be complete if armed groups remain intact indefinitely. Pursuit of universal disarmament, however, must be guided by reason.

I am confident that the decommissioning issue will not become an obstacle to progress for, in the context of the potential of a political agreement, when viewed in the round, it is unlikely that the Ulster Unionists will go to the wall over it. But the experience of increasing violence is an unsettling matter. While the support for those engaged in these attacks is small, they understand that acts of violence have a disproportionately severe impact on stability in our society. They may be insignificant in number but the threat they pose is far from insignificant. The bomb attacks by Republicans, which devastated two Protestant towns, and the murder of a Protestant man by the INLA at the weekend, have had a serious impact on confidence within the Unionist community.

It is thus not surprising that my community is far from optimistic about the chances of resolving the conflict, when there is actually more Republican violence now than at any time in the peace process. And there is growing concern that, as the political agreement takes shape, it is becoming increasingly uncertain that Sinn Féin will endorse the final product, meaning no doubt that the IRA would enter the fray again, just as it did in February. It is apparent that further fragmentation is already fomenting. Thankfully, the gardaí and the RUC have had considerable success in thwarting a number of Republican attempts at mass carnage. If the tons of explosives that they have intercepted had reached their targets, the situation might well have been very different than it is today. It is vital that the security forces in both jurisdictions concentrate on removing this threat from our society lest it derail our best efforts at this crucial time.

So, in nine days, we will all be in a new phase of the process, one way or another. I certainly hope that we can overcome the massive hurdles and beat the odds but, even if we do, there must not be any sense of complacency. An agreement does not translate easily into a settlement. That is an ongoing process, which can only be achieved over a long period of time through the successful application of the agreement and the institutions it will create.

Mistake to Interpret Agreement as a Settlement

(*Ireland on Sunday* April 5, 1998)

With only days left before the deadline for negotiations, some of the more contentious issues such as cross-border institutions made it back onto the agenda. This resulted in a hardening of positions of the parties within the talks as
well as increased pressure from those parties critical of the negotiations.

The prospect of reaching an agreement by next Thursday
is looking less likely than before. Over the past week, as the
negotiations have become almost intimate, the extent of the
division over some topics has been laid bare. The chances of
narrowing that ground enough to make our differences bridgeable is restricted by the short time still available. Even though
the negotiations have been intensified and are continuing
through the weekend, four days aren't much to work with.

While there are many obstacles to overcome, the greatest
one is how relations between a Northern Ireland Assembly and
the Republic of Ireland can be developed in a format acceptable to all sides. At this time, I believe that the Irish government fails to understand the scope for such a relationship, which
would be tolerable to the Unionist community. It is this area of
the negotiations which will probably make or break the agreement. So, unless the Irish government can adopt a realistic
approach, the process will fail. Progress is, however, being made
on the necessary alterations to the Irish constitution and that
will, of course, remove one of the hindrances to exploring better relations between our jurisdictions.

I feel that there is a fair chance of agreement on the structures for the new Assembly in Northern Ireland. It is tending
toward a legislative body founded on an executive structure
with shared responsibility. Satisfactory working arrangements
can be agreed and, in my view, concerns about the potential for

one community willfully to stymie its operation can be allayed. Its success will in a large part depend upon the creation of a Northern Ireland bill of rights, which provides a common protective safeguard.

Equally, the creation of a Council of the Isles, bringing regions together to cooperate on areas of mutual benefit, can draw fairly widespread support. It would be an all-encompassing mechanism to deal with the totality of relationships throughout the islands, within which the North–South relationships can exist in the appropriate context.

Issues such as the release of political prisoners are also intrinsic to the process, and must be satisfactorily resolved. I have made it clear consistently throughout the course of the peace process that the delicate and emotive issue of returning the prisoners of war to their communities was one of the more difficult but also most central areas to be addressed. Loyalists would find it impossible to endorse a political agreement that did not incorporate a program for action on prisoners. They have been a crucial component in the drive for a resolution of the conflict and that must be recognized in the agreement.

The task over the next few days is daunting but, if posturing is replaced by realism, it is possible – though not at this stage probable – that we can bring it together. But no one should make the mistake of interpreting an agreement as a settlement. The next two years will be infinitely more difficult than the last two, for the real test of viability for the peace process will be measured by the success of the implementation and operation of the agreement over an extended period.

I do not see the outcome of the talks as a transitional arrangement, but the description of the final settlement. Bertie Ahern's suggestion that there should be border polls every five years is extremely unhelpful in this respect. The agreement must have an opportunity to settle, rather than ensuring that the parties in the Assembly are on constant referendum footing. If the structures are not given the space to bed in, then they will be in a perpetual state of turmoil, with the communities constantly jarring against each other.

In the first instance, there will be parties like the DUP inside the institutions with a wrecking agenda, intent on making the Assembly unworkable. Sinn Féin is not likely to endorse the agreement because of its ideological restrictions to agreeing to Northern Ireland structures, and will probably not take its seats for the first year or so. That being the case, our work is cut out for us and further complications are unnecessary and unwelcome. Every effort must be made for the components of a potential agreement to be carefully screened for efficacy, lest we make the mistake of devising arrangements which may fulfill the political requirements of the various sides but are not suitable to meet the practical challenges upon application. In many ways, no deal is better than a bad deal. So let's make sure we get it right first time.

Proud to Be Associated with Defining Moment in History

(*Ireland on Sunday* April 12, 1998)

On April 10, after days and nights of intense negotiations, agreement was finally reached between Unionists, Nationalists, Loyalists and Republicans in Northern Ireland. The violent conflict, which had erupted in 1969, had finally come to an end.

Friday's talks agreement represents a defining point in Ireland's history, which may be the blueprint for a settlement. I am proud to be associated with an agreement that is the result of many years' work. My colleagues and I have invested a significant portion of our lives in the quest for a peaceful resolution of the conflict. We have moved on to the next stage of the settlement process, and must consolidate the work which has already been done by successful implementation of all aspects of the agreement. Only through the passage of time will we be able to assess the prospects of creating a permanent peace and of finally putting the conflict to rest. I sincerely hope that can happen, but peace is not just around the corner. It is entirely likely that we will experience some initial disharmony and trauma as our divided community grapples with the challenges of managing power and responsibility in a Northern Ireland Assembly.

There will continue to be opponents of the peace process, and people who will seek through various means to undermine our efforts. In all societies, there are those who resist political evolution. We must not allow the opponents of the peace process to exploit the uncertainty that undoubtedly exists throughout the community, either by terror or political persuasion. It is vital that the people of Northern Ireland are focused on embracing the opportunity of a new settlement, and have the leadership they require to move into a new era.

I have been involved in the negotiation process for two years, trying to establish a route to a profitable political agreement. There have been many twists and turns during that time and we have gone through both dark spells and periods of hope. Often it has been difficult to find a way through. As we entered the last stages of the negotiations this week, it was by no means certain that an agreement could be harnessed. The last days of the talks were characterized by sporadic rushes of activity interspersed with lengthy periods of tedious inactivity as one might have to sit back and let some of the parties concentrate on focused areas of difficulty.

The final two days took on a momentum in which the negotiations went into overdrive, particularly when Tony Blair and Bertie Ahern arrived. The world's media descended on Stormont and imposed additional pressure upon the proceedings. The level of optimism swung like a pendulum as seemingly impenetrable hurdles emerged and then were circumvented, only to be replaced by more. Negotiation was taking place around the clock and, when we eventually struck the deal, I had not slept in two days.

A fundamental problem was how to crack the nut on cross-border relationships. The initial draft agreement went far beyond the scope of the parameters of the talks and had to be seriously remodeled to pave the way for negotiation in other areas. It is impossible to engage in discussion at a late stage on proposals that are too far outside the margins of acceptability. The Irish government was well aware, after two years of dialogue on this matter, just how flexible Unionism could be on North–South relations. Yet, it insisted that the proposals should not reflect a compromise position, rather a singularly Nationalist position. The Irish government's bloody-mindedness almost destroyed the talks. That was why we dug our heels in until the draft proposals were reshaped before we would continue.

I must admit that I found it difficult to be optimistic at any stage, for the goal always seemed to be in the far distance. On Thursday night, I was telling the media that we had to prepare ourselves for the possibility that the differences between the parties might not be bridgeable. I had my last meeting with Tony Blair at four o'clock on Friday morning and I was far from convinced that we could make it. The final draft was presented to the parties at 11:30 on Friday and there was no indication even then that we would be able to agree on it. We had real problems with areas of it. Our delegates pored over the contents while munching on Kentucky fried chicken, which we had to send out for because the caterers had actually run out of food by this last stage of the marathon.

The question was whether the proposals could be accepted as a package, despite the difficulties we had with some of them. The plenary session, which would endorse or reject the document, was put off indefinitely until all of the parties could decide their positions. We eventually agreed that we would run with it at 4:00 p.m., but there were still negative sounds coming from the Ulster Unionist Party. It was apparent that their team had differences over the document. David Trimble finally made his decision and at 4:50 we were summoned to a plenary. Just after 5 p.m. a new chapter in Northern Ireland's history was opened. Time will tell whether the right decision has been made, though I believe it has. The public will ultimately interpret the Agreement in terms that will determine our success when they vote in next month's referendum.

I do not see the agreement as ideal, probably no party will, as there are components in it which still make me uncomfortable. However, I think that we took it as far as we could, trying to span the gaps. I am sure that the Unionist community will be uncertain about elements of the Agreement, but I am satisfied that Unionism's core principles have been upheld in this deal. Finally, we are removing the Anglo-Irish Agreement which has caused so much division, and the territorial claim over Northern Ireland will be removed from the Irish constitution. That clears an obstacle to a more constructive relationship between our jurisdictions. Northern Ireland's status as a member of the United Kingdom has been recognized by the Republic and its constitutional position underpinned by consent.

Structures will be created which will give the people of Northern Ireland unprecedented control over their affairs without external impediment, bringing with it a responsibility to exercise government. These structures will ensure that every person in Northern Ireland can play a full and equal role in society, and that there is equality of opportunity. New relationships will be explored throughout Ireland and across the British Isles with the creation of structures for cooperation which span the totality of relationships. Other key issues are being addressed, with a release program for political prisoners, and the creation of adequate rights protection. Nationalists will, of course, also see measures that will be important to them in the deal. What is crucial is that, while none of us is particularly ecstatic about the arrangements, we all are comfortable with them and recognize them as a compromise.

The next few weeks will be difficult, as we commend the fruit of our endeavors to the people who will be the final critics. If a substantial majority of the people endorse the package at referendum, then we will have created something wonderful. If, however, they do not, then we must commit ourselves to revisit the problem and try even harder. Personally, I firmly believe that it will be the former.

Postscript

The last days of negotiation had been intense and frustrating, the pressure immense. The deadline of midnight on Thursday had come and gone, and most of the time was spent waiting for others, interspersed by sporadic bursts of activity. The periods of inactivity were unbearable. The few hours immediately prior to the final plenary were excruciating as the Ulster Unionist Party leadership was locked in its rooms while a last minute coup unfolded. Jeffrey Donaldson, Member of Parliament for Lagan Valley and a principle negotiator, had tried to pull the carpet from under Trimble. The UUP parliamentary group was split down the middle over the Agreement proposals and was threatening mutiny if Trimble signed up to them. This was an ambush of the worst kind. Most of the UUP's members of parliament had played no role in the negotiation process and, in my opinion, had no interest in achieving a negotiated settlement. Donaldson, however, had been centrally involved in the talks. He chose to oppose Trimble at the last minute and publicly lambasted the proposal over the prisoner release, decommissioning and policing elements of it. But we suspected his eleventh hour antics were more to do with an ambition to undermine Trimble for self-gain than a matter of principle. He was fully aware of what had been taking shape over a period of months and therefore nothing in the proposals could have been of surprise to him.

At 5 p.m. on Good Friday the talks participants convened in the negotiating chamber to affirm their endorsement of the Agreement. This was the most historic moment in each of our lives. For some of us, it was not just the culmination of two long years of negotiations but the closing of a chapter in our lives that had stretched over many years of hard work. As the chairman, Senator Mitchell, finished his remarks, he opened the proceedings for each of the parties to state its position on the proposed Agreement and for the leaders of the groups to make brief comments. Every party in the room endorsed the proposal with the exception of Sinn Féin, which deferred its judgment.

When it was my turn, I adopted a more cautious tone than those who had spoken before me. I spoke of the difficulties we had overcome to reach this point and said that I should have felt exhilarated by our achievement. We had come farther than anyone had before in the search for a political settlement. But I did not feel exhilarated. What I felt was trepidation because I thought the times ahead would be even more challenging than what we had contended with up until then.

The Referendum

The outcome of the negotiations was the construction of a broad package that we hoped would be able to move our society closer toward peace and political stability. But the success of our efforts over two years of negotiation would ultimately be gauged by the people. The Stormont Agreement was a set of proposals that depended upon the endorsement of the people of Northern Ireland and the Republic of Ireland, within whose jurisdictions the package would be implemented. If the people rejected our efforts, then the package would be worthless. This was the ultimate test of the leadership of those parties in the negotiations. Would the people endorse our interpretation of what they would accept?

The referendum held in Northern Ireland on May 22, 1998 yielded 71.12% support for the Stormont Agreement. The campaign had been bitterly fought and those that led the charge for a No vote, while defeated, had succeeded in causing a deep rift within the Unionist community. Nationalism endorsed the Agreement overwhelmingly while only around 55% of Unionists voted Yes. A referendum was held simultaneously in the Republic of Ireland, which produced an expected 98% Yes vote.

Since the DUP and UKUP had left the talks the previous autumn, they had been energetically trying to prevent a positive conclusion to the talks process, and they vowed to attack any agreement that might emerge. They had made up their minds about the Agreement eight months before it existed and were prepared to oppose the deal regardless of what it contained. Unfortunately, they were able to exploit successfully the fears and uncertainty felt by many Unionists who found themselves susceptible to their scare tactics. The Agreement was portrayed as the end of the Union if it was to be implemented and those of us who had negotiated it were classed as traitors. We had "sold Ulster out" if Dr. Paisley and his colleagues were to be believed.

While we had been negotiating, the anti-Agreement forces had been preparing their campaign and they hit the ground running, launching a sophisticated and well-financed No campaign almost immediately after the talks had concluded. They found allies among dissident members of parliament in the Ulster Unionist Party who had challenged Trimble in the last hours of the negotiations. They depended on twisted lies and half-truths to project the contents of the Stormont Agreement as a cluster of concessions to Republicans. The emotive aspects of the package were isolated and elevated, the thrust of the No campaigners concentrating on the issues that were certain to raise hackles and rub raw nerves.

The two most contentious issues were the release of political prisoners and the likely qualification of representatives of Sinn Féin for ministerial positions in government. The first issue was understandably emotive. We had always held the view that those incarcerated for political offenses were political prisoners and should be released as part of the conflict resolution process. However, many people disagreed, and found this a very difficult issue to deal with.

At all times, we were sensitive to the feelings of victims of violence and, in fact, during the final stages of the negotiations, we had been openly critical of the lack of recognition for victims contained within the emerging package. Often the mistake is made of considering the issue as if there are two homogenous and separate groups in this argument. On one side there are the armed groups, the offenders, if you like, and on the other side there are the victims of violence. The reality is that the thread of hurt and trauma is woven throughout the community. We were arguing for prisoner releases but, at the same time, even among those who supported that position, deep anxiety and hurt had to be faced in doing so. Loyalist families, who had relatives in prison, wanted them to be able to come home after the end of the conflict. But Republicans in prison, who had killed or injured other members of those same Loyalist families, would be released also as part of the Agreement. This was hard for some of the families to deal with. I myself had to face up to the probability that those who had murdered my father and my friends would never be brought to justice because of the new situation I had helped to devise. That was difficult to accept but I believe that, although it was unsettling for a great many people, the release of prisoners was important and necessary as part of the package and in the long-term interest of the peace process.

I recall that, in the early hours of the morning on Good Friday as we contended with the last stage of negotiations, Sinn Féin sent representatives to our offices and to those of the PUP. There had been no individual contact between Sinn Féin and ourselves since they had been in the talks and we were surprised to see them at our door. My colleagues looked on as I uncomfortably went outside into the corridor to find out what they wanted. They thought that the terms included in the draft on prisoner releases could be improved if the UDP, the PUP and Sinn Féin were to harden our positions. It had been proposed that, if the groups with whom prisoners were associated were still on ceasefire two years after the release scheme had begun, all those still remaining in prison would be released. Sinn Féin reckoned that, with enough pressure, that could be reduced to a timescale of one year or eighteen months.

We did not go along with the proposal. Not only did the idea of reversing our policy and entering into deals with Sinn Féin at this late stage go against the grain, but we viewed prisoner releases as something that should assist conflict resolution and contribute to the healing process. If we pushed too far on this emotive issue, we were likely to obstruct the healing process and unjustly exacerbate the anguish felt in society. The different elements of the overall package had to form a carefully crafted balance that satisfied both the political and conflict resolution dimensions of the process, while not pushing the whole project beyond the parameters of public acceptability.

The other contentious issue was the potential for Sinn Féin to occupy seats in the new Northern Ireland government. For many people in Northern Ireland, and not just in the Unionist community, the prospect of having the political representatives of the IRA actually sitting in government was impossible to stomach. The strength of feeling that comes from thirty years of being on the receiving end of Republican terrorism is difficult to dispel. As part of our campaign for a Yes vote in the referendum, we engaged in a series of public meetings at which we offered an explanation of the contents of the Agreement proposals. Copies of the proposals had been sent to every household in Northern Ireland, but that did little to aid the Yes campaign. It was a complex document that was very difficult to read and most people did not read it closely, relying instead on the sweeping interpretations offered by political spokespersons. That did not work in our favor because the proposals could only be properly viewed in the context of their entirety and, therefore, it was difficult to compete against the selective elevation of provocative elements by our opponents who wanted to play on people's emotions. I had approached Mo Mowlam immediately following the final plenary of the talks and urged her to consider having a layman's guide to the Agreement drawn up to explain it in plainer language. Otherwise, we were going to be up against a barrage of willful misinterpretation by the No campaigners. She could not do this because it might be seen as the government trying to put a spin on the document.

I found during the public meetings that many of those who attended were already heavily influenced by the simplistic emotional interpretations offered by the No camp. While we were only able to expose relatively small numbers of people to the facts about the contents of the Agreement, once it was explained in its entirety and the different elements were placed in context, many people were able to take a more pragmatic view. But the one aspect that still caused the greatest resistance was that the adoption of proportionality meant it was likely we would have Sinn Féin as part of a government.

We had been long-time advocates of proportionality and the principle of collective responsibility. That meant that those parties that have a sizable mandate would have a reasonable chance of qualifying for a share of the positions of responsibility in the new institutions. Many people were supportive of the concept of proportionality but, when they had to face up to its full implications, they recoiled. They knew that it made sense but they could not come to terms with the reality of the IRA's representatives benefiting from it.

There were objections to Sinn Féin having a role in government while the IRA had not disarmed. We were opposed to disarmament being used as a sanction against any party and, in any case, the objections were not really about decommissioning *per se*. They were symptoms of more fundamental matters of lack of trust and confidence. The distrust with which the IRA and Sinn Féin were viewed was a result of experience, and the decommissioning issue, while used as a political blocking mechanism by some, was at one level a manifestation of the failure to overcome the chasm of suspicion.

I argued that people should examine the implication of Republicans conforming to a democratic settlement founded on the principle of consent and having to cooperate in a Northern Ireland Parliament within the United Kingdom. The reality of Sinn Féin taking its place on the same basis as others in a Northern Ireland Assembly, and particularly in positions of responsibility, was that Republicans would be compelled to participate in the administration of the "occupied six counties" that they had sought to obliterate. They had failed to destroy that community. Now they would be asked to work on its behalf. It was clear in our view that the Agreement demanded a far greater modification of position by Republicans than any other group. But a lot of people we spoke to were blinded by their anathema to the idea of Republicans in government.

It was apparent that this was an issue that would not be dealt with easily. It was going to be a hurdle of monumental proportions to overcome and it was to prove a fundamentally contentious issue when the Assembly was formed later in 1998. I believed that the onus was on Republicans to prove themselves to those who distrusted them if they were to overcome this obstacle.

The Assembly Elections

The elections, which took place in June 1998, were a severe disappointment because they became almost a re-run of the referendum. One might have hoped that the strong overall endorsement of the Agreement proposals the previous month would have influenced a shift in the attitude of the public. What actually happened was that the proximity between the April Agreement, May referendum and June election became a seamless period and, therefore, the issues remained unchanged. People were not interested in the practical and social issues that candidates presented to them. They did not vote on the basis of those who would most accurately represent their needs on the daily issues that would affect their lives during the first term of the first Northern Ireland government for twenty-seven years. Instead, they voted on a pro-Agreement/anti-Agreement basis. At least, within Unionism that was what happened. There was very little opposition to the Agreement within Nationalism and, therefore, the Nationalism battle was a more conventional one for supremacy between the SDLP and Sinn Féin.

The most serious split was in urban working-class areas. We knew when we had argued over the electoral system during the negotiations that the UDP, along with other small parties, was going to find it hard to compete, particularly in Unionist areas, where the electorate was being offered a proliferation of Unionist parties. In fact, the last round of negotiations we had at the talks had been on the electoral system. The division that emerged over the Agreement affected our chances even more seriously. We found that working-class areas were heavily split and that was where our vote was going to come from. In the end, we failed to have a representative elected to the Assembly. The best opportunity we had was for me in Lagan Valley but, while my vote was significant, I did not make the cut.

One reason for this was what became known as the "Donaldson factor." Jeffrey Donaldson had asked for dispensation to stand as a candidate for the Ulster Unionist Party but his request had been declined. In my view, it would not have been appropriate to have a primary candidate campaigning against the policy of his own party, but it did get him a lot of sympathy because it was presented as censure. Quite a few people who would have voted for the UUP decided to move their support over this issue. And, while they were not comfortable supporting Ian Paisley, the quasi-intellectual image which Bob McCartney of the UKUP projected became a happy home for these tactical dissenters who gave their votes to McCartney's candidate in Lagan Valley, Paddy Roche. Roche had also had private meetings with representatives of the local Orange Order to elicit support among its members and supporters. The unlikely performance of Roche pushed him way ahead of what anyone anticipated and he effectively closed off my chances.

The UDP's image had also been negatively affected by circumstances earlier that year. Two particular events come to mind. The first was our suspension from the negotiations that January. We were excluded from the talks because the UFF had broken its ceasefire, retaliating against INLA and IRA murders of Protestants. The second was during the referendum campaign when Michael Stone, one of the most prominent UDA political prisoners, attended a public rally that we had organized to call for a Yes vote. He had been released from prison for a number of days as part of a normal parole procedure but the No campaign asserted that he had been let out specifically for our rally and that this was a concession to paramilitarism. That was not true for we had made no request for his release. The situation was not helped by the fact that the government had, in fact, released the IRA's Balcombe Street gang from prison the previous weekend to attend Sinn Féin's annual conference.

Michael Stone attended the rally, as was his right to do so. He was and is fully committed to the success of the peace process and the removal of violence forever. But we knew his presence would be sensationalized, exploited and taken out of context. I believed that he had every right to be there but that it was unwise to come. It turned out a PR disaster. His presence gave encouragement to elements of our constituency but damaged how others in wider society viewed the UDP. And the media focused solely on Michael, ensuring that the message from the speeches was lost completely.

The result of the Assembly election was not only a personal disappointment but also, as a whole, did not produce what Northern Ireland deserved. The sizable minority of anti-Agreement members diminished the chances of success of the new Assembly, which was meant to take society forward into a new political era. Moreover, the isolation of a significant section of Loyalism from the next stage of the peace process presented serious problems. The UDP had spent a considerable number of years dedicated to a strategy of moving society beyond conflict, working to create the environment that could allow political progress to take shape. Now, having played such a central role in the peace process and the creation of the Northern Ireland Assembly, we failed to have representation in it.

As is the case for Sinn Féin and the PUP, our relevancy to the success of the peace process stretches far beyond our electoral mandate. Of course, Sinn Féin refuses to acknowledge that that is the case with its party and hides behind its mandate, while everyone else accepts its importance is because it represents the IRA. Part of the essential ingredients of successful conflict resolution are the transition from physical force to non-violent political expression and the creation of stable political structures. The UDP took a conscious decision to encourage those in the Loyalist community who had resorted to armed conflict that there had to be the room to develop an alternative option. Someone had to take on that role, and it was not going to be the UUP or DUP; so we did.

We had had considerable success. Loyalists called a unilateral ceasefire for the duration of the Brooke Talks in 1991, despite having no political representation there. In 1994, the second Loyalist ceasefire coincided with the first IRA cessation. The opportunity existed for the first time to move the conflict into a completely political dimension and grasp the challenge of seeking an agreed way forward for our divided community in a non-violent atmosphere.

The discussions on that way forward could not succeed unless there was a peaceful atmosphere and, to ensure that was the case, it was important that all sides understood what was taking place and had a means to influence or participate in the process as it developed. In 1991, Loyalists put their trust in politicians who would not communicate with them, and called a ceasefire on the basis of trust, without having an influence on or complete knowledge of what was taking place behind the closed doors of the talks. They were let down and that was not going to happen again.

Clearly, it was not going to be acceptable for armed groups to sit around the table with all others directly because, while that has been the case in other conflict resolution processes, ours is not that kind of conflict or society. So there had to be a way to ensure that Loyalists were aware of what was taking place in the negotiations and were in a position to contribute to it, albeit in a roundabout manner. We became that vehicle. It has never been a case of armed groups dictating the agenda but rather a commonsense attitude toward trying to bring everyone along the road to peace.

The theory went somewhat askew when the IRA revoked its ceasefire in 1996 and went back to terrorism. That seriously destabilized the peace process and could have led to a full resumption of armed conflict that would have made the process unsalvageable, but the convening of negotiations in June of that year provided an alternative course to the predictability of cyclical violence. I do not believe that Loyalists would have resisted the challenge to re-engage in conflict with the IRA but for the fact that they saw the negotiations as a genuine opportunity for us to find another way forward and, for the first time, have the Loyalist voice heard within such a process.

The IRA's provocation was not heeded because Loyalists saw the negotiations as a route towards addressing the problem in a truly comprehensive fashion. I think that particular period of the peace process provided the greatest challenge to Loyalists. It tested the success of our endeavors to the extent that the paramilitaries had the choice either to revert to type and react to IRA violence as they had instinctively done in the past, or to resolve to hold their nerve and put faith in our ability to provide leadership within the talks in the hope that we might move the process forward, isolate the IRA and possibly force them to re-instate the ceasefire by seeing that they were being left behind. The judgment of the Loyalist leadership was that they would serve their community and their ideals better by contributing to the search for a settlement. Although this is a rather simplistic analysis, it is in effect what really happened between 1996 and July 1997. The IRA came back on board because they had failed to hold the talks back and found themselves left with no other choice.

Loyalists did regress when the UFF broke its ceasefire following the IRA and INLA murders of Loyalists at the beginning of this year, but that round of sporadic violence was short-lived. We exerted all our influence at that time to recover the situation before it spiraled out of control. Our success was repaid by an expulsion from the talks (a much longer expulsion than that applied to Sinn Féin when the IRA's contribution to that violence was exposed.)

In April 1998, we had finally succeeded – against all odds in securing an Agreement in the negotiations. That Agreement was formally supported by the UFF, the only paramilitary organization to do so. The fact that its support was declared, despite the clear division within Unionism and in a context where there was no compulsion to take a public stand, is an example of the UFF's strength of commitment to the peace process and its genuine intent finally to move beyond conflict. If we had not performed the perhaps unpopular role we did in making sure that the Loyalist perspective was integral to the peace process and the negotiations, the process would not have come as far as it did.

Now, unfortunately, as we entered the next and most challenging stage of the process, that of putting the products of our negotiations into practice and trying to make them work, a significant part of Loyalism had been cut loose. While the UDP failed in this instance within the framework of the electoral process, our relevancy can no more be measured exclusively against our electoral strength today than it could at the start of the peace process.

There are obvious problems inherent in having the largest Protestant combatant in the conflict isolated from the peace process. We were extremely sensitive to the dilemma posed by our failure to gain representation. I found that being unanchored from the process in this way led to a gradual reduction of influence on the Loyalist paramilitaries. Of course, I do not mean to suggest that, because we did not make the cut, Loyalists were suddenly likely to end their ceasefire.

The major future difficulty I foresaw was the potential for the anti-Agreement forces to gain more power as a result of a negative reaction to the Assembly elections and, in particular, the chance that isolation would lead to misinterpretation as highly charged issues dominated the early stages of the Assembly's life. The political electricity discharged by issues such as disputes over parades would parallel the emotive issues which caused rancor among the parties on the inside of the Assembly and division among the communities on the outside. Unlike in the past, Loyalists did not have an attachment to the democratic process or an avenue to contribute to the debate or, more importantly, an accurate insight into the goings on in the Assembly, but rather found themselves on the outside, listening to the emotive rhetoric of the most vocal and extreme elements of Unionism. The challenge presented by all of this made it imperative that the UDP did not lie down in the face of this adversity but battled against the tide to ensure that corruption of support for the Agreement was minimized.

Making the Agreement Work

It was clear from the outset that huge problems were going to emerge as the Agreement was implemented. The fledgling Assembly hit trouble the moment it was created, with a dilemma over the allocation of ministerial posts dominating debate. The first act of the Assembly had been to elect David Trimble First Minister, effectively the Prime Minister of Northern Ireland, and the SDLP deputy leader, Seamus Mallon, as Deputy First Minister. For months to follow, these two gentlemen held the only official positions in the Assembly as the formation of other internal structures was delayed.

As the Agreement devised the Assembly as a collective government with the make-up of its Executive proportionally reflecting the make-up of the Assembly, Sinn Féin was entitled to two ministerial posts. Predictably, there was huge resistance to allowing Sinn Féin to occupy these posts because the IRA had made no move toward disarmament. Indeed, Trimble refused to form the Executive until Republicans had decommissioned while Sinn Féin insisted that disarmament was not a condition for the allocation of ministerial positions. The impasse that subsequently emerged threatened the timetable for implementation of the Agreement. The deadline set for the establishment of the Executive and other structures had been October 31, 1998. The target date came and went without progress. The Assembly remained in "shadow" form while its structures and procedures were established and preparations were made to get it up and running. While it was not going as planned, the impasse would not represent a crisis unless it disturbed the formal empowerment of the Assembly. It was unlikely that Westminster would transfer powers to the structure while there was no executive mechanism in place.

In order for the impasse to be broken, a compromise of some sort would be required. The principal players in the equation were Trimble and Gerry Adams. Both appeared to be in genuine tight spots. For Adams, concessions on decommissioning could put the IRA's support for the peace process on the line. The IRA's membership had been given assurances that weapons would not be surrendered. Trimble, on the other hand, risked losing members of his own party and, consequently, the pro-Agreement majority among the Unionist representation in the Assembly. The absence of my party meant that the UUP and PUP held the slenderest of majorities as the only pro-Agreement Unionists in the Assembly. Within the UUP, there were people who were shaky and could not be trusted to hold the party line.

At the time of writing, the impasse has still not been resolved but I expect some route will have been found to circumvent the immediate danger of a collapse of the Agreement. Keeping the peace process alive and making the Agreement work are sure to be the constant challenges faced as the people of Northern Ireland contend with the search for a lasting settlement. The Stormont Agreement does not represent a settlement in itself; it merely provides a new landscape that may be exploited to achieve eventual peace. The careful construction of the Agreement redefined the relationships between the peoples of Northern Ireland, the UK and the Republic of Ireland. We devised a framework that both reflected the democratic will of the people of Northern Ireland to remain within the UK and also ensured that the historic divisions with the Republic of Ireland were replaced with a constructive relationship to match the political realities of this modern age. This was complemented by the provision of safeguards that protected the rights of all traditions in Northern Ireland and allowed us to work together in our common interest by sharing the responsibility to govern and to facilitate a process of normalization that would remove the trappings of conflict. This represented a fundamental and comprehensive package for change which, we believed, offered a reasonable opportunity to redefine our society.

But merely having reached agreement on the package and having begun to implement it did not guarantee that it would cure our collective ills. The Agreement is not worth its weight in spit if it cannot command the support and confidence of the community. The success of the peace process does not depend on the creation of clever formulas for government, but on our ability to achieve an evolution in the attitude of society that enables it to override the emotions that have led to division and to be at peace with itself. That will take a long time and requires a strong relationship between the new institutions and the community as a whole.

It can be seen in other conflict areas where new democratic systems have emerged that, because those elected have become focused on the difficulties of adapting to a new political situation and to making the institutions work, the community has inadvertently become isolated from the overall peace process. If that were to happen in Northern Ireland's case, it would be disastrous. Those within the community who already feel opposed to the Agreement or the direction of the peace process would have their opposition reinforced while enthusiasm among supporters of the process would wane. It is crucial that the institutions of governance do not grow apart from the people.

One problem is that there has always been a gap in the relationship between the political and community levels of society. Direct rule has kept power out of the hands of local politicians. Consequently, the political agenda that guided the performance of parties has been determined primarily by sectarian and ethnic alignments of those parties. Because of the nature of the conflict, political leaders have largely stayed away from social issues over which they have no control.

As a result, political parties have not developed a close working relationship with community bodies and regard them as a bit of a nuisance and of secondary concern to national identity issues. On the other hand, the community sector is largely skeptical of politicians and views them as a selfish elitist group detached from the grassroots and unconcerned about bread and butter issues. Unless this chasm is bridged, the Assembly will grow apart from the community, further undermining ownership of the process.

It is very likely that the impact of the transfer of power into local hands will actually promote greater alienation, particularly within the working class. We all share some blame for playing the politics of the opposition, where it is easy to be critical of government policy because we do not have to make those decisions. For thirty years, we have blamed successive Labor and Tory governments for the ills inflicted on our society but the hard decisions over health cuts and education will now be taken by local politicians, and I am not sure that the community will react well to that. As the politicians grapple with handling power and applying policy, it is likely that there will continue to be a decline in social conditions. This time, the community will blame its own politicians, and become more detached. Only by overcoming the ownership gap can the community be educated to empathize with the difficulties faced by the new administration and equally develop a stronger social awareness among its representatives to cushion the impact of the fundamental shift in responsibility that is underway.

As part of the Stormont Agreement, a Civic Forum was to be established comprising representatives from the voluntary and business sectors and the labor movement. The idea was pushed primarily by the Women's Coalition within the negotiations and aimed at including civil society in the workings of government. There was no great level of enthusiasm for the proposal among the larger parties at the talks but it was finally included in the package. But it was clear that the Civic Forum was viewed as a minor concession to inclusivity and that there was very little chance of the UUP or SDLP giving it much emphasis. By the end of 1998, the details of how it would operate and its relationship with the Assembly had not even been considered. Effectively, it was not a priority area for Trimble and Mallon who were facing enough problems trying to get the main structures up and running. Yet, if the Civic Forum was formulated properly and given real meaning, it could be a vehicle to promote greater social inclusion and a greater sense of ownership among the grassroots.

The Future of Loyalism

A lot has been achieved over the past few years since the peace process became public, and we have come farther as a society than any of us could have expected. Our objectives in the process for Loyalism have been to bring an end to war and to create conditions for an eventual political agreement that would provide mutual respect in spite of our differences and ensure fairness and equality of treatment for all sections of Northern Irish society. If you say it quickly, it does not sound like much. In order to do this, we have had to persuade our own community that there is a viable alternative to further conflict and that we could be a fluent voice for Loyalism. We have had to force others to acknowledge the legitimacy of the Loyalist community's aspirations and to understand the parameters of a comprehensive settlement. We have had to contend with severe opposition and division within our own community.

I cannot recall any one instance where the road ahead seemed unobstructed; my colleagues and I have shared many doubts and apprehensions along the way, but we have, in my belief, succeeded in nudging our society forward. Each mountain we have set out to climb has seemed insurmountable but, with perseverance, some obstinacy and a lot of luck, we managed to scrape through. I was not sure we could convince the CLMC to end its military campaign in 1994, but we did. I would be lying if I said I had been confident that the ceasefire would hold during the pensive period when the IRA resumed its terror campaign, but we got through it. During the first eighteen months of the negotiations, I did not believe that it would be possible to bring about a positive conclusion to the talks, and even in the final stages I was not sure it would work.

Today, I am still not sure it will stick. I am, however, absolutely firm in my belief that the Agreement which we did finally broker represents a good deal for my community. Indeed, it represents a fair deal for all sections of society. For thirty years, Republicans have sought to force political change by the use of violence and, in return, Loyalists have been compelled to resist by force. For a quarter of a century, the people of Northern Ireland have had decisions affecting their lives taken by governments that were not elected by them and that have shown themselves consistently to be untrustworthy. My community has been denied effectual political leadership and has been historically discriminated against by the political elite.

Now we have a very different landscape. Republicans have had to face up to the reality that their so-called armed struggle has been futile. They have accepted a new political arrangement that recognizes the rights of the Unionist tradition and demands that Republicans conform to democratic principles. The Agreement makes the traditional Republican strategy, to force the British government into political change in Northern Ireland regardless of the peoples' wishes, irrelevant. Future political change requires Republicanism and Nationalism to seek the consent of Unionism. The viability of an armed struggle has been removed.

Even the unfortunate exclusion of the UDP from the Assembly has in one peculiar way been an advantage, in so much as it forced us to consider the concept of alienation in a broader context. Our own sense of isolation allowed us to step back and look at the developing process from a distance. It made me focus on the issues of ownership and confidence within the community from a perspective that made it clear that we had to help tackle the division between the Assembly and the community, consolidating the peace process on the ground among the grassroots.

The Loyalist community has new options for political representation in the form of parties such as mine and we have proven that Loyalism can make a strong impact at the highest political levels. We have shown that there is a place for working-class voices in the political arena, although we have been limited because of emotive exploitation of the working class over the merits of the Agreement by Paisley and his doomsday brigade. That can be reversed by the determination of the UDP to encourage strong proactive grassroots leadership in Loyalist areas and to continue to strive for greater accountability in government on social issues that affect the working class most directly.

The future is, of course, somewhat uncertain for the UDP because we are not represented in the Assembly but that is a temporary set back. We will not give up the struggle to secure social and political recognition for the Loyalist people. Loyalists will have their voice heard with clarity and understanding because they will do it themselves from a position of equality and respect. And the UDP will be there to make it happen.

Chronology

1966
Ulster Volunteer Force re-established and outlawed

1967
February 1 Northern Ireland Civil Rights Association (NICRA) formed

1970
April 30 "B" Specials dissolved
IRA split into Official and Provisional IRA
SDLP founded under the aegis of Gerry Fitt and John Hume

1971
September Ulster Defense Association (UDA) formed, uniting a number of Loyalist groupings
Democratic Unionist Party (DUP) founded by Ian Paisley
Internment re-introduced until 1975

1972
January 30 Bloody Sunday. Fourteen people attending a demonstration in Londonderry against internment killed by British soldiers. British army alleges its soldiers had returned fire from snipers
March 24 British Conservative Prime Minister Edward Heath announces dissolution of Stormont government. Northern Ireland to be ruled directly from Westminster
IRA resumes bombing campaign in Britain

1973
November 22 Newly elected Northern Ireland Assembly announces Unionist–Nationalist power-sharing Executive. December Conference at Sunningdale to discuss how to address conflict; excludes Loyalists
Ulster Freedom Fighters (UFF) formed
Ireland and UK join EEC

1974
March 23 Loyalist Ulster Workers' Council (UWC) threatens strike action and civil disobedience unless new assembly elections held
May 15 UWC strikes begin
Sunningdale Agreement and Assembly collapse

In Birmingham, six Irish people, protesting their innocence, arrested for bombing that killed twenty-one people. Finally released in 1991

1980
April 1 Special political status removed from all Loyalist and Republican prisoners
October 27 Republican hunger strikes begin

1981
March 1 Republican prisoner Bobby Sands goes on hunger strike in H-Blocks of Maze Prison
April 9 Sands wins Fermanagh-South Tyrone Westminster by-election
May 5 Sands dies. In all, ten Republican prisoners die
Ulster Loyalist Democratic Party (ULDP) formed
Anglo-Irish Intergovernmental Council established

1982
IRA bombs in London's Hyde Park and Regent's Park, killing ten people

1984
IRA bomb Grand Hotel, Brighton, venue for Conservative Party Conference, killing five people
Report of New Ireland Forum published

1985
November 15 Signing of Anglo-Irish Agreement at Hillsborough Castle by Margaret Thatcher's Conservative government and Garret FitzGerald's Fine Gael/Labor coalition. It stipulated that there should be no change in constitutional position of Northern Ireland for so long as the majority wishes to remain as part of United Kingdom. However, it drew strong opposition from Unionist community. 200,000 people marched on Belfast City Hall to show their anger
Ulster Clubs formed by John McMichael and Allen Wright to bring together Unionists and Loyalists

1986
March 3 General strike in protest against the Anglo-Irish Agreement
July IRA declares that any civilian working for security forces is a legitimate target
November Large protest gathering at Belfast City Hall for anniversary of Agreement

1987
January "Commonsense" Document published by UDA. First considered political proposals to emerge from Unionism in response to Anglo-Irish Agreement. Proposes a Northern Ireland Assembly with a bill of rights and consensus government

July 2 Report of DUP and UUP task force, examining alternatives to the Agreement

November 8 IRA bomb kills eleven people and injures 63 during war remembrance service. Among the dead, Gordon Wilson's daughter Marie. His eloquent words of forgiveness urge all sides to peace

December 22 UDA political strategist John McMichael killed in IRA booby-trap bomb

1988
March 11 UDA chairman Andy Tyrie resigns

October 14 Exploratory two-day discussions among DUP, UUP, SDLP and Alliance in neutral venue of Duisburg, West Germany

ULDP re-established

John Hume intensifies economic and political outreach to the USA. Holds secret talks with IRA

1989
May ULDP in its first democratic elections; Ken Kerr elected as local councilor in Londonderry. By year end, ULDP changes name to UDP

September 14 Cambridgeshire Deputy Chief Constable John Stevens appointed to investigate possible collusion between British security forces and Loyalist paramilitaries. Leads to arrest of several senior UDA personnel

Sinn Féin publishes its proposals for resolution of the conflict in policy document "Towards a Lasting Peace"

1990
January 2 UDP member Harry Dickey killed by under-car booby-trap bomb

Sir Peter Brooke, British Secretary of State for Northern Ireland, declares that Britain no longer has any selfish economic or strategic interest in Northern Ireland

1991
April 30 Unilateral Loyalist (CLMC) ceasefire for duration of Brooke Talks between UUP, DUP, SDLP, and Alliance

June 29 IRA shoot dead UDP North West Chairman Cecil McKnight

July 3 Brooke Talks and Loyalist ceasefire collapse

IRA fire mortar bombs into garden of the British Prime Minister's residence at 10 Downing Street

1992

Sir Patrick Mayhew becomes British Secretary of State for Northern Ireland. Mayhew Talks last six months and involve the Irish government

One hundred pounds of IRA semtex explodes at the Baltic Exchange in London. Gerry Adams loses his seat in Westminster

1993

May IRA two-week ceasefire

September 25 Hume–Adams joint statement

October 23 IRA bomb fish shop on the Shankill Road, killing ten and injuring 57 people. By end of month, Loyalist gunmen had retaliated by killing twelve people, seven of them in a bar in Greysteel, County Londonderry. Gerry Adams carries coffin of IRA man Thomas Begley who killed himself in the Shankill bombing

October 29 Joint Communiqué in Brussels by British and Irish governments repudiating Hume–Adams peace initiative

December 15 British–Irish Joint (Downing Street) Declaration. UDP approached for secret talks by Irish government. Reject proposal. CLMC set out six principles as basic parameters for an accommodative settlement

1994

July 11 UDP Chairman Ray Smallwoods shot dead

August 28 Hume–Adams joint peace statement; followed by statement from Taoiseach Albert Reynolds

August 31 IRA ceasefire

September British Prime Minister John Major visits Belfast

October 13 CLMC announces ceasefire, expressing "abject and true remorse" for the suffering of victims of the conflict

October 28 Forum for Peace and Reconciliation begins in Dublin Castle

November 16 Irish Labor party withdraws from Albert Reynolds' government

December 5 Fianna Fáil and Labor negotiations broken off. John Bruton of Fine Gael becomes Taoiseach in coalition government with Labor and Democratic Left (These two left parties merge in December 1998)

December 13–14 Economic conference in Belfast hosted by John Major

1995

February 22 Launch of New Framework Document for Agreement by British and Irish governments. Rejected as a basis for negotiation by all Unionist parties.

March 1 In Washington, Irish Foreign Minister Dick Spring warns that waiting for an IRA surrender or decommissioning is a "formula for disaster"

March 17 St. Patrick's Day celebrations in the White House. UDP first Loyalist party to attend. Sinn Féin fund-raising ban lifted

May 24–27 Economic investment conference on Ireland hosted by President Clinton in Washington's Sheraton Hotel

June British governments renew anti-terrorism laws

July 3 Private Lee Clegg, jailed for murder of Belfast teenager Karen Reilly in 1990, released after serving two years of his sentence

July High tension and demonstrations during marching season, particularly at Ormeau Road in Belfast, at Drumcree, and at Garvaghy Road in Portadown

August 12 Apprentice Boys march in Londonderry for 25th anniversary of Battle of the Bogside, despite strong Nationalist protest

August 25 CLMC state that there would be no first strike from Loyalism, that its weapons were for defense only

September David Trimble elected to succeed James Molyneaux as leader of UUP. UDP and Sinn Féin share speaking platform for the first time

September 18 UDP holds talks with Irish Premier John Bruton in Dublin. Heralds the first meeting between Loyalists and an Irish Taoiseach

November 28 Downing Street Joint Communiqué by British and Irish governments launching a "twin-track" approach and outlining all-party talks by end of February 1996. They propose an International Body to investigate decommissioning

November 30 President Clinton visits Belfast and Londonderry

1996

January 22 Mitchell Report on decommissioning published but sidelined by Unionists and Tories in favor of elections

February 9 Breakdown of IRA ceasefire: Canary Wharf bombed, killing two and injuring over a hundred people

February 28 John Bruton and John Major meet in London and announce all-party talks for June 10

March Festivities at White House. Sinn Féin excluded. UDP choose to stay away. David Trimble applauded for being first Unionist to attend. Taoiseach John Bruton pleads with IRA to renew ceasefire

March 21 Procedures and date for Northern Ireland elections announced, and plans for Northern Ireland Forum

May Sinn Féin agrees to Mitchell Report and its six principles

May 30 Elections for political party representatives to Northern Ireland Forum; Sinn Féin wins 15.47% of total poll or seventeen seats. The PUP and UDP win 2 seats each

June 10 Multi-party talks begin, excluding Sinn Féin. Senator George Mitchell finally accepted as chairman on June 12

June 15 Arndale shopping center in Manchester bombed by IRA

June 28 IRA mortars fired at British army barracks in Osnabrück, Germany

July 8 LVF murder Catholic taxi driver Michael McGoldrick amid Loyalist rioting

July 11 RUC reverse their decision of July 6 to ban Garvaghy Road Orange march in Portadown. Nationalist rioting

July 12 Lower Ormeau Road in Belfast under curfew for twenty-six hours

July 14 Killyhevlin Hotel bombed in Enniskillen; later, Republican Continuity Army Council (CAC) admit responsibility for the attack

August After last-minute negotiations, Apprentice Boys agree to redirect annual march on Londonderry's city walls in order to prevent confrontation

September 23 Large finds of IRA arms and explosives in England

October John Hume and Gerry Adams present further peace proposals to British government

November 11 Cross-party and community delegation visits site of Battle of the Somme as memorial service to commemorate the Northern and Southern Irish dead in Great War, and those killed in conflict closer to home

November 15 Sinn Féin outlines pre-conditions required from British government in order to achieve re-instatement of IRA ceasefire

1997

February 12 IRA killing of British soldier Bombardier Stephen Restorick at Bessbrook, County Armagh

March Large attendance by Northern Ireland parties at White House St. Patrick's Day celebrations

May 1 British general election; Labor party sweeps to power, ending eighteen years of Tory rule

May 21 Local government elections in Northern Ireland. UDP wins four seats, from holding only one since 1993 elections

June New Labor Prime Minister Tony Blair visits Belfast

June British government publishes decommissioning policy document agreed with Irish government

June 6 Republic of Ireland elections

June 16 Two RUC constables Roland Graham and David Johnston shot dead in Lurgan by IRA

June 28 Alban Maginness installed as first Catholic Belfast Lord Mayor

July 1 Taoiseach Bertie Ahern and Northern Ireland Secretary of State Mo Mowlam meet to discuss the proposals on decommissioning

July 6 High tension at Garvaghy Road where Orange march forced down despite strong Nationalist protest. Orange Order unilaterally abandons or re-routes seven other contentious parades

July 20 Restoration of IRA ceasefire

September 9 Sinn Féin enters negotiations, accepting Mitchell Principles. Two days later, IRA rejects Principles. DUP and UKUP withdraw from talks

September 15 Multi-party talks resume, with Senator George Mitchell as chairman

December 27 LVF leader Billy Wright shot dead in Maze Prison by INLA

1998

January Mo Mowlam visits Maze Prison to hear Loyalist prisoners' views as they threaten to withdraw support for talks

January 19 Loyalist Jim Guiney shot dead by INLA

January 26 UDP excluded from talks due to UFF murders

February Sinn Féin excluded from talks due to IRA murders of Brendan Campbell on February 9 and Loyalist Robert Dougan on February 10

March 3 Friends Catholic Damien Trainor and Protestant Philip Allen shot dead by LVF in Poyntzpass, County Armagh

March Northern Irish politicians visit White House. Belfast City Council organizes its first St. Patrick's Day celebration

March 19 Violent exchanges between DUP and UDP at a DUP anti-peace process rally in Lisburn

March 23 UDP and Sinn Féin back in talks for substantial negotiations on strands one, two and three

April 10 Agreement finally reached on Good Friday in hours after April 9 deadline set by Senator Mitchell

May 22 Referenda take place in the Republic and in Northern Ireland. Overwhelming vote in both jurisdictions in favor of the Good Friday Agreement. The Agreement aims for a power-sharing executive Assembly to be based at Stormont, greater awareness of human rights, a review of policing, institutes a North–South council and a British–Irish Council to promote greater cooperation throughout the British Isles

June 25 Elections to 108-member Northern Ireland Assembly. In tight voting, UUP win majority of seats, while SDLP come second. Next largest groupings are Gerry Adams' Sinn Féin party and Ian Paisley's DUP. In gathering of Assembly, UUP leader David Trimble voted First Minister, and SDLP deputy leader Seamus Mallon elected Deputy First Minister

July For fourth consecutive year, high tension surrounds traditional Orange parade in Drumcree. Newly appointed Parades Commission bans parade but Orange Order hopes to defy ruling, which it claims is unlawful. RUC barricade Unionists from walking traditional route

July 11 Three small boys burned to death when house torched in largely Loyalist estate in town of Ballymoney. Their Catholic mother survived

August 15 A massive bomb explodes in busy shopping street in Omagh, County Tyrone. 29 people killed; many more badly injured. A group calling itself the Real IRA admit that it was their attack. Shortly afterwards, the group calls ceasefire

September 3 US President Bill Clinton visits Belfast, Omagh and Armagh. Pledges his continuing hopes in and support for peace process

September 14 Stormont Assembly inaugural meeting. 4 minutes silence maintained for Omagh victims. Unionist parties object to Sinn Féin holding positions in the Executive of the Assembly before the IRA has decommissioned its arms. Four members of David Trimble's UUP announce that they disagree with their leader working alongside Sinn Féin and are forming a new party, to be called the United Unionist Assembly Party

October 31 Deadline for establishing Executive passes without progress

December 18 Agreement reached on Executive structure, to comprise ten government departments and six cross-border implementation bodies

LVF start decommissioning of their weapons

Biographies

David Adams UDP negotiator, Lisburn Borough Council member

Gerry Adams Leader of Sinn Féin party 1983–

Bertie Ahern Taoiseach 1997– . Leader of Fianna Fáil party 1994–

Lord John Alderdice Presiding Officer (Speaker) of Northern Ireland Assembly. Former leader of Alliance Party 1987–98

Sir Hugh Annesley Former RUC Chief Constable 1989–96

Tony Blair British Prime Minister, 1997– . Leader of British Labor party 1994–

Sir Peter Brooke Secretary of State for Northern Ireland 1989–92

John Bruton Leader of Fine Gael party 1990– . Taoiseach 1994–1997

John de Chastelain Canadian army general and member of 1995 international decommissioning body. Chairman of body overseeing implementation of decommissioning

Dr. Robin Eames Primate of the Church of Ireland

Garret FitzGerald Leader of Fine Gael 1977–87. Taoiseach 1981–82 and 1982–87. Signed Anglo-Irish Agreement with then British Prime Minister Margaret Thatcher

Ronnie Flanagan RUC Chief Constable 1996–

Edward Heath British Conservative Prime Minister 1970–74. Signed Sunningdale Agreement of December 1973

Hari Holkeri Former Norwegian Prime Minister. Member of 1995 international decommissioning body

John Hume Leader of SDLP 1979– . Member of European Parliament. Joint winner of Nobel Peace Prize in 1998 for his work on bringing peace to Northern Ireland

Martin McGuinness Sinn Féin MP for Fermanagh-South Tyrone

Cecil McKnight North West chairman of UDP. Shot dead in his home June 29, 1991

John McMichael (1948–87) Politically active Loyalist. Co-wrote the UDA "Commonsense" Document. Father of Gary McMichael. Killed by an under-car booby-trap bomb outside his home December 22, 1987

Ken Maginnis MP for Fermanagh. UUP security spokesperson

John Major Former British Conservative Prime Minister 1990–97. Signed 1993 Downing Street Declaration

Seamus Mallon Deputy First Minister of Northern Ireland Assembly 1998– . Deputy leader of SDLP

Sir Patrick Mayhew Former Secretary of State for Northern Ireland 1992–97. Former British attorney general

George Mitchell former US senator and chairman of 1995 international decommissioning body. Chairman of all-party talks leading to Good Friday Agreement

James Molyneaux Former leader of the Ulster Unionist Party 1979–95

Dr. (Marjorie) Mo Mowlam British Secretary of State for Northern Ireland 1997–

Rev. Ian Paisley Set up the Free Presbyterian Church in 1951. Founder and leader of the Democratic Unionist Party 1971– . MP for North Antrim since 1970

Albert Reynolds Former Taoiseach and leader of the Fianna Fáil party 1992–94. Signed 1993 Downing Street Declaration. Instrumental in ceasefire negotiations with John Hume and Gerry Adams

Peter Robinson Deputy leader of DUP

Bobby Sands (1954–81) IRA prisoner in Long Kesh. Went on hunger strike for political status. Died after 66 days. Elected as MP during his strike

Ray Smallwoods (1950–1994) Chairman of UDP. Brought about the 1991 Loyalist ceasefire. Shot dead July 11, 1994

Dick Spring Leader of Irish Labor party. Former Tánaiste and former Minister for Foreign Affairs. In coalition government with Fine Gael 1981–2 and 1982–87, with Fianna Fáil 1993–94 and with Fine Gael and Democratic Left 1994–97

Margaret Thatcher British Conservative Prime Minister 1979–90. Signed the Anglo-Irish Agreement in 1985 with then Taoiseach Garret Fitzgerald

David Trimble First Minister in Northern Ireland Assembly 1998– . Leader of Ulster Unionist Party 1995– . Joint winner of Nobel Peace Prize in 1998 for his work on bringing peace to Northern Ireland

Andy Tyrie Former chairman of UDA. Resigned in 1988

John White UDP negotiator

Glossary

Alliance Party Moderate, reformist, Unionist party in Northern Ireland, set up April 21, 1970. Formerly led by Lord John Alderdice. Currently led by Sean Neeson

Anglo-Irish Agreement Document agreed to by the Fine Gael–Labor coalition in Dublin and Margaret Thatcher's Conservative government in London in 1985. Signed at Hillsborough on November 15. It stipulated that there should be no change in the constitutional position of Northern Ireland for so long as the majority wishes to remain as part of the United Kingdom. However, it drew strong opposition from Unionists

Anglo-Irish Intergovernmental Conference Forum for the British and Irish governments to meet at regular intervals to discuss the affairs of Northern Ireland; recommended in the Anglo-Irish Agreement

Árd Chomhairle National Executive

Árd Fheis Annual Party Conference

Articles Two and Three of the Irish Constitution These two provisions of the Irish constitution, dating from 1937, described the national territory as constituting the island of Ireland, and were cited by Unionists as the major hurdle to their cooperation with the Dublin government in any talks concerning the future of the North. They were amended by referendum in accordance with the 1998 Good Friday Agreement. The definition of territory is now based on the idea of who is entitled to be part of the Irish nation

Bloody Sunday January 30, 1972. Fourteen people attending a demonstration in Londonderry against internment were killed by British soldiers

"B-Specials" Controversial Unionist state militia first formed in 1920 as a back up force for the police. Disbanded and reformed as the Ulster Defense Regiment (UDR) in 1970. This in turn was disbanded and replaced by the Royal Irish Regiment (RIR) in July 1992

Combined Loyalist Military Command (CLMC) Umbrella grouping of militant Loyalism, including UDA, UFF, UVF and Red Hand Commando

"Commonsense" Document Political proposals by UDA in response to Anglo-Irish Agreement. It advocated the creation of a Northern Ireland government, devolved from the British parliament

Continuity Army Council (CAC) Small break-away Republican paramilitary group

Conservative Party (Tory Party) Britain's main right of center political party. Allied with the Ulster Unionist Party in Northern Ireland

Craic Fun

Decommissioning Body Set up in December 1995 to investigate the difficult issue of decommissioning arms

Democratic Unionist Party (DUP) Extreme right-wing Unionist party, formed in 1971, led by Rev. Ian Paisley

Direct Action Against Drugs (DAAD) Vigilante-style organization to combat crime. Believed to be a front for IRA activity

Downing Street Declaration Statement issued December 15, 1993, by the British and Irish governments. Set out principles around which the two governments would seek a settlement for Northern Ireland

Easter Rising Rebellion in April 1916, primarily in Dublin, seeking the establishment of an independent Irish Republic. Led by Pádraig Pearse, James Connolly and others. The outcry at the execution of the leaders in the aftermath led eventually to the War of Independence 1919–21. The Anglo-Irish treaty of December 6, 1921 brought about the Northern Ireland state

European Union (EU) 15-member economic union. Founded in 1957. Ireland and the UK joined in 1973 when it was known as the EEC

Fianna Fáil Founded in 1926 by Eamon De Valera; the largest of the Irish political parties, led by Bertie Ahern

Fine Gael Formed in 1933, the second largest political party in the Irish Republic, led by John Bruton

Forum for Peace and Reconciliation A consultative body set up in Dublin Castle on October 28, 1994, by then Taoiseach Albert Reynolds. Its remit was to consult on and examine ways in which a lasting peace, stability and reconciliation could be established by agreement among all the people of Ireland. Its final report was published February 2, 1996

Framework Document Published on February 22, 1995 by the British and Irish governments, it outlines the parameters as agreed between the Dublin and London governments for a talks process

Good Friday Agreement Published on Friday April 10, 1998 after extensive all-party talks in Northern Ireland, and including the British and Irish governments. Aims for more cross-border cooperation, greater awareness of human rights, and institutes a North–South council, a British–Irish Council, as well as a power-sharing executive Assembly to be based at Stormont. Stipulated changes in Articles Two and Three of Irish Constitution

Hume–Adams Initiative A political initiative undertaken in talks between John Hume and Gerry Adams, after an initial contact in January 1988. It led to a joint statement in September 1993, outlining the right of national self-determination, the importance of earning the allegiance of the different traditions on the island, and placing the responsibility of framing all-party talks on the Irish and British governments

Internment The imprisonment of dissidents without trial in Northern Ireland. Used in 1922, 1939, 1956 and 1971–75, and applied principally against Republicans

Irish National Liberation Army (INLA) Republican paramilitary group

Irish Republican Army (IRA) Title given to original Irish Nationalist militant group which fought the British after the establishment of the first Dáil (Irish parliament) in 1919. Divided into the Official IRA and the Provisional IRA (Provos) in 1969

Joint Declaration See "Downing Street Declaration"

Irish Republican Socialist Party (IRSP) Small Republican paramilitary group

Labor Party (Ireland) Third largest political party in the Republic of Ireland, founded in 1912, formerly led by Dick Spring. Currently led by Ruairí Quinn. Merged with the Democratic Left party in December 1998

Labor Party (UK) Britain's main left of center political party, led by Tony Blair

Loyalism Belief in loyalty to the British Union. Unionists who use violence to achieve their ends are often described as Loyalists, although not all Loyalists support political violence. Traditionally made up of working-class sections of the Unionist community

Loyalist Volunteer Force (LVF) Loyalist paramilitary group, formerly led by Billy Wright until his murder in December 1997

Member of Parliament (MP) Elected political representative of UK parliament which meets at Westminster in London

Mitchell Principles Six key principles set out in the Mitchell Report on Decommissioning, published January 22, 1996

Nationalism Belief in establishing a united nation encompassing all of Ireland

Northern Ireland Civil Rights Association (NICRA) Set up February 1, 1967 to fight against discrimination. Identified as Republican and therefore opposed by Loyalists

Orange Order (Orangemen) Name taken from the victory of Protestant William of Orange over Catholic King James II. A powerful secret sectarian order of Protestants whose pageantry is perceived by Nationalists as supremacist

Parades Commission Set up in 1997 to rule on routing of individual parades, or whether they should take place

Progressive Unionist Party (PUP) Loyalist political party, led by David Irvine. Links with UVF

Republicanism Political ideology born out of the French and American revolutions. Believes in the right of Irish people as a whole to determine the future of Ireland. Seeks a democratic, non-sectarian, pluralist society – a thirty-two county Irish Republic

Royal Ulster Constabulary (RUC) Paramilitary state police force in Northern Ireland; rejected by most Nationalists

Social Democratic and Labor Party (SDLP) Nationalist and second largest party in Northern Ireland, founded in 1970, and led by John Hume

Sinn Féin "We Ourselves" or more commonly translated as "Ourselves Alone." Irish Republican party founded in 1905, and led by Gerry Adams. The only party substantially organized both in the North and in the Republic of Ireland. Links with IRA

Stormont Seat of the Unionist government and parliament from 1932 to 1972, when direct rule from Westminster was re-established. Venue for the new Northern Ireland Assembly

Sunningdale Agreement Signed in December 1973 between the British Conservative government of Edward Heath and the Irish government led by Liam Cosgrave. Established a power-sharing government and Council of Ireland. It lasted five months and was brought down by vigorous Unionist opposition

Tactical Use of Armed Struggle (TUAS) IRA definition of their strategy between 1994 and 1996 ceasefires

Tánaiste Irish deputy Prime Minister

Teachta Dála (TD) Member of Irish parliament (Dáil)

Taoiseach Irish Prime Minister

Twelfth of July Commemoration of the Battle of the Boyne every year by the Orange Order, part of the "marching season." In recent years, violent clashes have occurred when the loyal orders seek to march along their traditional routes through Catholic areas

UK Unionist Party (UKUP) Small Unionist party, led by Bob McCartney

Ulster Nine-county province of ancient Ireland. However, the term is now commonly used by Unionists to refer to the six counties in Northern Ireland

Ulster Defense Association (UDA) Founded in September 1971, the major Loyalist paramilitary group, now outlawed

Ulster Defense Force (UDF) Loyalist paramilitary training group created in 1986 by UDA

Ulster Democratic Party (UDP) Founded in 1988 as ULDP (changed name in 1989), led by Gary McMichael. Links with UDA

Ulster Freedom Fighters (UFF) Loyalist paramilitary group

Ulster Loyalist Democratic Party (ULDP) Former name of UDP. First formed by John McMichael of the UDA in 1981. Re-established in 1988

Ulster Unionist Party (UUP) Largest Unionist party, led by David Trimble, also known as the Official Unionist Party

Ulster Volunteer Force (UVF) Originally formed in 1912 to oppose Home Rule, re-established in 1966 and is now a banned Loyalist paramilitary group

Ulster Workers' Council (UWC) Loyalist organization founded to generate wide-scale strike action and civil disobedience in protest against the Sunningdale Agreement

Unionism Belief in maintaining the 1800 Act of Union with Britain. Unionists are traditionally from the middle-classes of the Protestant community

Index